THE AMERICAN BAR ASSOCIATION

GUIDE TO

WORKPLACE LAW

Other books by the American Bar Association

The American Bar Association Guide to Consumer Law
The American Bar Association Guide to Family Law
The American Bar Association Guide to Wills and Estates
The American Bar Association Guide to Home Ownership
The American Bar Association Family Legal Guide

THE AMERICAN BAR ASSOCIATION

GUIDE TO

WORKPLACE LAW

Everything You Need to Know
About Your Rights as an Employee
or Employer

 TIMES BOOKS

RANDOM HOUSE

Points of view or opinions in this publication do not necessarily represent the official policies or positions of the American Bar Association.

This book is not a substitute for an attorney, nor does it attempt to answer all questions about all situations you may encounter.

Copyright © 1997 by American Bar Association

All rights reserved under International and Pan-American Copyright Conventions. Published in the United States by Times Books, a division of Random House, Inc., New York, and simultaneously in Canada by Random House of Canada Limited, Toronto.

Library of Congress Cataloging-in-Publication Data

The American Bar Association guide to workplace law / the American Bar Association.—1st ed.
    p.   cm.
  Includes index.
  ISBN 0-8129-2928-4
  Cover title: ABA guide to workplace law.
  1. Labor laws and legislation—United States—Popular works.
I. American Bar Association. II. Title: ABA guide to workplace law
KF3319.6.A46   1997
344.73'01—dc20
[347.3041]   96-35913

Random House website address: http://www.randomhouse.com/

Printed in the United States of America on acid-free paper

9 8 7 6 5 4

Design by Robert Bull Design

AMERICAN BAR ASSOCIATION

■

v

Victoria L. Bor
Sherman, Dunn, Cohen, Leifer &
  Yellig
Washington, D.C.

John F. Burton, Jr.
Dean
School of Management and
  Labor Relations
Rutgers University
New Brunswick, New Jersey

Donald W. Cohen
Asher, Gittler, et al.
Chicago, Illinois

Beth Gaudio
Howell, Gately, Whitney &
  Carter
Towson, Maryland

Robert W. Gilbert
Gilbert & Sackman
Los Angeles, California

Jay Grenig
Professor of Law
Marquette University Law School
Milwaukee, Wisconsin

Linda H. Lamel
Vice-President
TIAA/CREF
New York, New York

Sorrell Logothetis
Logothetis, Pence & Doll
Dayton, Ohio

Adrianne Mazura
Rudnick & Wolfe
Chicago, Illinois

Robert K. McCalla
McCalla, Thompson, et al.
New Orleans, Louisiana

Gloria M. Portela
Seyfarth, Shaw, Fairweather &
  Geraldson
Houston, Texas

Theodore St. Antoine
Degan Professor of Law
University of Michigan Law
  School
Ann Arbor, Michigan

Jules Louis Smith
Blitman & King
Rochester, New York

John T. Subak
Dechert, Price & Rhoads
Philadelphia, Pennsylvania

CONTENTS

Foreword   xi

Preface   xiii

Introduction   xv

CHAPTER ONE: How Law Affects the Workplace   3
*From Government Regulation to
Private Agreements*

CHAPTER TWO: The Hiring Process   14
Ads, Tests, Interviews—and More

CHAPTER THREE: Terms and Conditions of Employment   39
*Everything from Wages to Sexual
Harassment, Leave Time, and Health
Insurance*

CHAPTER FOUR: Ending the Employment Relationship   78
Leaving Your Job—Voluntarily or Not

CHAPTER FIVE: Retirement   97
Your Pension and Social Security Rights

CHAPTER SIX: Unions in the Workplace   106
Rights for Both Workers and Employers

CHAPTER SEVEN: Government Employment   128
*Civil Service, Constitutional Protections,
and Other Special Features*

CHAPTER EIGHT: Enforcing Workplace Rights   138
*Guidelines for Resolving Workplace
Problems*

APPENDIX I: Defining the Terms Found in
Federal Law   149

APPENDIX II: Labor and Employment Laws   154

Index   181

CONTENTS

FOREWORD

Howard Vogel, *Chair*
Standing Committee on Public Education

WORKPLACE LAW AFFECTS ALMOST EVERYONE in this country. Obviously, most adults work at wage-paying jobs, and so are directly affected by the laws and rules that touch on everything from minimum wages to leave time. But millions of retirees are also affected by workplace law governing their pension rights. And the spouses and dependents of workers could be directly affected by laws covering health benefits, as well as indirectly by the laws affecting workers.

Both employers and employees are at a big disadvantage if they're not familiar with the law of the workplace. Since the New Deal, workers and companies have been increasingly governed by law. Just about every aspect of the employment relationship is covered, from the first day on the job to the last (and possibly beyond in the case of retirement and health benefits, to say nothing of severance pay, noncompete agreements, and references).

In plain language you can understand, this book looks at everything from avoiding discrimination in hiring to avoiding sexual harassment on the job. It looks at all the issues relating to unions, and the special considerations affecting government workers. It suggests steps for resolving workplace problems quickly and inexpensively, and if these steps fail, a comprehensive listing at the end of the book shows you how you can make use of the major federal laws on labor and employment.

To make this book as helpful as possible, we define all the key terms in everyday language, use plenty of examples drawn from ordinary life, and accompany the text with short articles highlighting additional points of interest.

Sometimes a problem is so complex, or so much is at stake, that you'll want to seek legal advice from someone who knows the facts of your particular case and can give you advice tailored to your situation. But this book will give you a solid grounding in workplace law that will help you whether you are an employer or an employee. Armed with the information in this book, you can be sure that the actions you take will be in your best interest.

SPECIAL ACKNOWLEDGMENT

We express our gratitude to the American Bar Association's Section of Labor and Employment Law, which took a particular interest in this project and facilitated a thorough review of the manuscript. The chair of the Section, Donald Paul MacDonald, appointed a five-person committee of Section leaders to review the manuscript. The committee consisted of Victoria L. Bor, Sorrell Logothetis, Robert K. McCalla, Gloria M. Portela, and Helen M. Witt.

Their careful review assured that the manuscript accurately and thoroughly covered this important subject. We thank the Section for its interest and involvement in this project.

Howard H. Vogel is the managing partner of a Knoxville, Tennessee, law firm. He is a former member of the ABA Board of Governors, and he served as President of the Tennessee Bar Association in 1995–96.

PREFACE

■

Robert A. Stein, *Executive Director*
American Bar Association

T HE AMERICAN BAR ASSOCIATION legal guides are designed
to provide guidance for people on important legal questions
they encounter in everyday life. When American families are asked
to describe their legal needs, the topics that come up repeatedly are
housing, personal finance, family and domestic concerns (usually in
conjunction with divorce and child support), wills and estates, and
employment-related issues. In addition, more and more Americans
have questions about operating a business, often out of the home.

These are the topics that *The American Bar Association Legal
Guides* cover in plain, direct language. We have made a special effort to make the books practical, by using situations and problems
you are likely to encounter. The goal of these books is to give helpful information on a range of options that can be used in solving
everyday legal problems, so that you can make informed decisions
on how best to handle your particular question.

The American Bar Association wants Americans to be aware of
the full range of options available when they are confronted with a
problem that might have a "legal" solution. The Association has
supported programs to eliminate delay in the courts, and has worked
to promote fast, affordable alternatives to lawsuits, such as mediation, arbitration, conciliation, and small claims court. Through ABA
support for lawyer referral programs and pro bono services (where
lawyers donate their time), people have been able to find the best
lawyer for their particular case and have received quality legal help
within their budget.

The American Bar Association Legal Guides discuss all these alternatives, suggesting the wide range of options open to you. We

hope that they will help you feel more comfortable with the law and will remove much of the mystery from the legal system.

Several hundred members of the Association have contributed to *The American Bar Association Legal Guides*—as authors and as reviewers who have guaranteed the guides' accuracy. To them—and to the ABA's Standing Committee on Public Education, which was the primary force behind the publications—I express my thanks and gratitude, and that of the Association and of lawyers everywhere.

Robert A. Stein is executive director of the American Bar Association. He was formerly dean of the University of Minnesota Law School.

PREFACE

INTRODUCTION

A T ANY GIVEN TIME, about half of all Americans—over 128 million—are earning wages. Most adults now work for wages or at some point will hold a wage-earning job. Thus, laws regulating the workplace potentially affect almost everyone. There are federal and state laws that touch on the whole employment relationship. How these laws affect either the worker or the employer depends on a lot of factors, including how many workers the employer has, the particular facts of the situation, the state in which the work is performed, and the type of job. Workplace law potentially covers everything from hiring to terms and conditions of employment to firing and other endings to employment. A basic understanding of what the law requires can help both the employer and employee develop realistic expectations, anticipate problems and avoid trouble.

This book describes federal and state labor and employment laws, detailing the rights and protections available to employees, the limitations placed on employers, and the ways of enforcing these laws. It provides an overview of the legal rights and duties that affect both workers and managers in the workplace.

We hope that this book will help you understand the legal environment of the workplace, whether you are an employer or an employee. We answer basic questions you might have about employment law, explain the application of the law in certain situations, and provide sources for obtaining additional information. This book will help employees determine if the law can help them resolve problems they encounter at work, and it will help employers determine if their policies are consistent with the law.

THE AMERICAN BAR ASSOCIATION

GUIDE TO

WORKPLACE LAW

■

CHAPTER ONE

How Law Affects the Workplace

From Government Regulation to Private Agreements

WE TALK ABOUT "THE LAW" of the workplace, but it's more of a patchwork quilt than a single fabric. There are many federal and state laws that cover different aspects of work, but they don't necessarily affect every business and every worker. For example, federal laws could apply to worksites all over the country, but they typically exempt businesses that employ fewer than a certain number of workers—and that number varies from law to law. It may be 15, or 20, or even 50. So if you work for a small business, you may be covered by some laws and not covered by others.

Maybe your state has stepped in to fill the gap by covering workers of smaller businesses—but maybe it hasn't. And perhaps your state has simply duplicated the federal provisions and applied them to workers like yourself, or perhaps it has expanded these provisions for workers in the state, giving you more protections (it can't give you fewer protections than federal law provides, as explained later in this chapter). Perhaps your locality has a law on the subject—or perhaps not.

Even when federal law does apply to your company, it does not regulate *every* aspect of the employment relationship. For example, federal law prohibits employers from discharging employees based on race, but it does not require employers to have just cause before firing someone. That means that as far as federal law goes most of us are what the law terms **employees at will.** We can be refused employment, be disciplined or fired for many reasons (or perhaps for no reason), even though federal and state laws make some reasons illegal.

And this is not all of "the law." These are just the **statutes,** the laws enacted by Congress, state legislatures, and local government. The law of the workplace is also affected by **employment contracts** between an individual worker and employer; an example would be a contract between a professional athlete and a team. More common are **collective bargaining agreements** between a company and a union. These can deal with everything from rate of pay to working conditions and protections against arbitrary dismissal. (Contracts like these usually give you protections and make you something more than an "at-will" employee.)

Then there is **case law,** the decisions of state and federal courts that interpret the law and serve as precedent for other courts. **Company personnel handbooks** may be a factor in a case, as might employer practices. If you're a government worker, **civil service rules** are probably a very important aspect of "the law."

At first glance, all this might appear to be very confusing, but don't despair. There are many sources of employment law, and much potential for confusion, but there's help too. This book will

---

WHO IS AN EMPLOYEE?

Before workplace laws can apply, there's the issue of whether you are an employee in the first place. The focus of this book is on the laws that regulate the relationship between employers and employees. We don't discuss laws dealing with **independent contractors,** who are not considered to be employees and don't have the benefit of the many laws that protect employees. (See "The Trend to Contingent Workers" on page 6 for why companies are turning to independent contractors.)

What is the difference between an employee and an independent contractor? One difference is that an employee gets a salary or wage, rather than being paid on a per project basis. Another is that an employee is furnished the equipment used in the performance of the work; the independent

---

take you through basic principles and situations that will help you understand how the law might affect you, whether as employer or employee. Appendix I defines key terms found in federal laws. As a ready reference, Appendix II of this book lists the major federal employment laws, grouped into categories, and tells you where you can find detailed information on particular laws.

And, as noted below, legislators are aware that it might be hard for workers to know about workplace laws, and have provided that key provisions of many laws must be posted at the workplace.

NOTICE POSTING

Many federal labor and employment laws (as well as many state laws) require employers to post notices at the workplace informing employees of their rights under the law. The notices must be posted conspicuously and in enough places so employees can see them as they enter and exit the workplace.

---

contractor supplies his or her own. A third difference is that an employer controls, directs, and supervises an employee in the performance of his or her work, whereas when an independent contractor is hired a company merely specifies the result to be achieved, and the individual uses personal judgment to achieve that result.

The following gives an example of someone who is an independent contractor and not an employee. Suppose ABC Company retains Jill to put up a fence for $1,000. ABC does not supervise Jill's work or give her tools or pay her a salary. It only wants to get its fence built. Jill wants profits, not wages and benefits. Her relationship with ABC ends after the job is done. Workplace law will not apply to the relationship of ABC and Jill, the independent contractor.

Companies can get official copies of such notices from the various federal agencies charged with enforcing the statutes. To ensure that

THE TREND TO CONTINGENT WORKERS

What business wouldn't want to cut down expenses for injuries, workers' compensation laws, and unemployment claims? How about lowering other employee expenses and lessening the impact of workplace laws?

Enter the **contingent worker**—the temp, the part-timer, the independent contractor. Jobs in these categories have grown faster than traditional full-time jobs in the past decade, and contingent workers now make up more than 25 percent of the workforce.

The trend is not surprising. Experts estimate that contingent workers cost from 20 to 40 percent less than full-time workers.

Part of the reason is that such workers aren't fully covered by workplace laws. Some observers feel that one purpose of corporate downsizing and outsourcing is to limit the impact of government regulation on a company by reducing the number of full-time employees and using more contingent workers, who have fewer legal protections.

For example, if they work less than a certain number of hours, part-timers are not subject to some laws, such as the Family and Medical Leave Act. In addition, using contingent workers instead of full-timers may keep certain businesses small enough to be exempt from certain workplace laws.

Some observers speculate that increased efforts to guarantee workers' rights have, ironically, contributed to the trend. By adding to employers' labor costs, workplace laws may encourage alternatives that provide fewer protections for workers generally.

The downside for companies is the considerable risk of lower morale on the job, reduced quality and productivity, and the need to seek and train workers constantly. When figuring in these factors, companies may conclude that the cost savings are illusory and they're better off with experienced, full-time employees.

they will remain prominently posted as required, and not get frayed, defaced, or lost, it is a good idea to post them in glass or clear plastic cases. To make sure they're noticed, they may be placed near time clocks and at the various entrances to the workplace.

FEDERAL LAWS

Federal laws will be discussed extensively throughout this book, and are summarized in Appendix II. Here is a quick list of some of the most important ones. The description following each law gives some indication of its content, but, of course, is not meant to be a detailed analysis. For that, turn to the appropriate chapter of this book, or consult a lawyer or employment law expert, who may also be able to discuss state employment laws in your state.

ANTIDISCRIMINATION LEGISLATION	*Title VII of the Civil Rights Act of 1964, as Amended* prohibits discrimination in employment based on race, sex, religion, national origin, or color.
	The *Age Discrimination in Employment Act* prohibits discrimination in employment based on age against persons who are 40 years of age or older.
	Title I of the Americans with Disabilities Act and the *Rehabilitation Act* prohibit discrimination in employment against persons with disabilities.
WAGES AND HOURS OF WORK	The *Fair Labor Standards Act* requires employers to pay employees a minimum wage rate per hour and to pay 1½ times the employee's regular rate for each hour over 40 worked during any given workweek; also imposes restrictions on the employment of children under the age of 18.
	The *Equal Pay Act* requires employers to pay equal wages to male and female employees who are performing substantially equivalent work.

WORKPLACE SAFETY	The *Occupational Safety and Health Act* requires employers to furnish a workplace free from hazards likely to cause death or serious injury and to comply with safety and health standards promulgated under the statute.
PENSIONS	The *Employee Retirement Income Security Act* establishes eligibility and vesting rights for employees in company pension plans, as well as administrative, fiduciary, funding, and termination requirements for pension plans.
IMMIGRANT WORKERS	The *Immigration Reform and Control Act* prohibits employers from hiring illegal aliens; requires employers to verify the work eligibility status of applicants; prohibits discrimination in employment based on citizenship status against lawfully admitted aliens.
UNION-MANAGEMENT RELATIONS	The *National Labor Relations Act* requires employers to engage in collective bargaining with unions designated by their employees, and prohibits discrimination in employment based on union activities or participation in protected concerted activity.
OTHER TERMS OF EMPLOYMENT	The *Uniformed Services Employment and Reemployment Rights Act of 1994* requires employers to reinstate employees who have served in the armed forces to their former jobs upon completion of their military duty.
	The *Worker Adjustment and Retraining Notification Act* requires employers to give 60 days' advance notice of plant closings or mass layoffs to workers, unions, and state and local governments.
	The *Employee Polygraph Protection Act* prohibits employers from requiring employees or applicants to submit to polygraph examinations.
	The *Family and Medical Leave Act* requires employers to grant employees up to 12 weeks of unpaid leave during any 12-month period because

of the birth or adoption of a child, because the employee has a serious health condition, or because the employee has to care for a parent, spouse or child with a serious health condition.

STATE LAWS

Most federal laws contain limitations in coverage. Besides applying only to employers of a certain size as determined by number of employees, some apply (or not) depending on the dollar volume of the company's business. Other laws, such as **Title VII** (a very important federal antidiscrimination statute), limit the categories entitled to protection—the law prohibits employment discrimination only if it is based on race, sex, religion, national origin, or color, but not if it is based on any other reason. And, of course, many aspects of employment are simply not regulated by federal law.

Many state legislatures have stepped in to fill possible gaps in workplace regulation. They've enacted statutes to expand the scope of coverage or provide additional protection. Thus, when you're confronted by a workplace problem, don't look just at federal law; try to find out if your state has a law dealing with the issue.

In the area of employment discrimination, for example, many states have enacted legislation that mirrors the protection offered by Title VII, the **ADEA** (the federal age discrimination law) and the **ADA** (the key federal law protecting individuals with disabilities from discrimination). These state laws might expand coverage to the smaller employers that do not meet the coverage requirements of the federal laws. Or they might add categories entitled to protection. Thus, federal laws protect employees on the basis of race, color, religion, national origin, sex, age, and disability, but some state laws also prohibit discrimination based on marital status, sexual orientation, or arrest record. The federal age discrimination law applies only to employees who are 40 or older, but many states prohibit age discrimination regardless of age.

In the area of union-management relations, many states have

enacted state-law versions of the **NLRA** (the main federal labor relations law), which apply to smaller employers not meeting the dollar volume necessary for federal law to apply. In some states, special agricultural labor relations laws regulate the union-management relationship of farmworkers who are excluded from the coverage of the NRLA. There is no federal law governing union-management relations of state and local government workers, but many states have passed laws granting government employees the right to be represented by unions and bargain collectively. In some states, all categories of government employees have these rights; in others, only limited classes of employees are given the right, such as police and firefighters or schoolteachers.

In the field of wage and hour laws and workplace health and safety, some states have laws that give you a higher level of protection than you get under federal law. For example, federal law currently requires employers to pay a minimum wage of $4.75 per hour; a few states, however, set a higher minimum wage in their state. Similarly, some state workplace safety regulations impose stricter safety and health standards than required by federal law.

States have also passed legislation dealing with issues that federal law has simply left unregulated. For example, there are state laws:

- prohibiting employers from discriminating against employees who have engaged in legal off-duty behavior such as smoking;
- requiring employers to give employees time off to vote in elections; and
- prohibiting companies from firing workers who "blow the whistle" on illegal corporate activity.

Two very important sources of worker rights—**workers' compensation laws** that pay employees for injuries incurred at work, and **unemployment insurance laws** that pay benefits to employees who have lost their jobs—are administered by the states.

Throughout this book, as we discuss workplace issues, we'll refer to the range of state laws that supplement federal statutes. While we can't detail the laws of each specific state, we do discuss state law generally and point out how it impacts upon the work relationship. It is rare for any two states to have laws exactly alike, however, so this book will not provide guidance on how any one specific state's laws affect the workplace.

THE RELATIONSHIP BETWEEN FEDERAL AND STATE LAW

Federal and state laws interact in four ways. In some circumstances, federal law **preempts** any attempt by states to regulate the same conduct. This means that a state cannot pass *any* law that regulates conduct already covered under federal law. In other circumstances the state is allowed to **supplement** or **extend** the protection found in federal law, as long as it does not undermine the rights given by federal law. Finally, a state can **regulate** if there is no federal regulation on that topic, or if some employers are not subject to federal law (because they do not meet the guidelines for coverage—for example, a retail establishment that grosses less than $500,000 a year is not covered under the NLRA). In these circumstances, a state can decide whether it will regulate the conduct and what the extent of that regulation will be.

Examples of Preemption Both the NLRA and **ERISA** (the main pension law) preempt any attempt by the states to regulate the activity covered by these federal laws. For example, the NLRA regulates how employees select unions to bargain collectively for them. A state can't require a labor union to register with the state before it can represent employees—such a state law is not enforceable because it is preempted by the federal regulation. Similarly, ERISA provides that after five years of service an employee is eligible for 100 percent of the pension benefits earned. A state is preempted from passing a law that would give an employee 100 percent of benefits after only three years of service.

Examples of Supplementing Federal Law. As a general rule, all other areas of federal labor and employment law allow states to supplement the protection provided under federal law. The federal law acts as a floor beneath which the state may not go, but allows the state to set a higher ceiling. For example, the **Family and Medical Leave Act (FMLA)** requires covered employers to provide 12 weeks of unpaid leave to employees in certain circumstances. State law could require that same employer to provide 13 weeks, or require the employer to provide paid instead of unpaid leave.

Examples of Extending Coverage. As we've seen, even when the federal government does regulate an issue, employers that are not covered by the federal law can be subjected to state laws that vary in content from the federal law. For example, the FMLA applies only to employers with 50 or more employees. A state, therefore, can pass family leave legislation covering employers with *fewer than* 50 employees. Thus, while the FMLA requires employers covered under the statute to provide a minimum of 12 weeks of unpaid leave, the state law could mandate that employers with fewer than 50 employees need only provide 4 weeks of unpaid leave (or are not required to give any leave at all).

Regulating Where There Is No Federal Law. When the federal government does not regulate an activity, the states are generally free to decide whether or not they wish to pass legislation covering that topic and what the extent of that regulation will be. For example, although there is a federal law that prohibits employers from discharging employees who are called to serve jury duty in federal court (**Jury System Improvements Act**), the law does not cover employees who are called to serve jury duty in state court. Therefore, some states have enacted legislation to deal with state court jury duty while other states have not.

State regulation may result not only from laws passed by the legislature, but also from state court decisions interpreting the **common law**. (The common law originated in England and was later applied to the United States; it is based on precedents set by courts and not on legislative enactments.) There is no federal law requiring employers to honor promises made in company manuals, for example, but some state courts have interpreted the common law of contracts as making such promises enforceable.

■

CHAPTER TWO

The Hiring Process

Ads, Tests, Interviews—and More

SEVERAL STAGES ARE USUALLY INVOLVED in hiring employees. First, an employer determines the qualifications that are needed to perform the job in question. Next, the employer circulates a job description, soliciting applications for the position. Last, the employer hires someone from among the applicants. The law impacts on each of these stages.

Most of these laws aim to prevent discrimination. We discuss antidiscrimination laws in the bulk of this chapter. But first, let's take a look at some other federal and state laws that may affect hiring. These laws are generally not as sweeping as the antidiscrimination laws. Rather, they usually impose conditions either for hiring certain types of employees or for working at certain types of jobs.

CHILD LABOR LAWS

The federal **Fair Labor Standards Act (FLSA),** which dates back to the New Deal, regulates the employment of **child labor,** limiting the conditions under which companies can hire children. "Child labor" applies to any individual under the age of 18. In order to comply with the FLSA, employers are required to set age limits for certain jobs.

As a general rule, companies cannot employ children under 14 years of age. There are three exceptions to this rule: minors working for a parent who is the sole proprietor of the business; minors working as actors; and minors working as news carriers.

Minors who are 14 or 15 years old can't work at all in certain hazardous occupations. Some occupations that are considered hazardous for these young people are: transportation; construction; mining; operating power-driven machinery; maintaining and repairing equipment; and working in and around a boiler room. The idea is to keep them from activities where they could be severely injured. Minors who are 14 or 15 can be employed in some retail and service-industry jobs.

Even if an employer can hire minors who are 14 or 15, the law limits the hours they can work. They cannot work during any hours when they are expected to be in school. They may work a maximum of 3 hours on a school day (up to 18 hours a week). On nonschool days, they can work for a maximum of 8 hours a day (up to 40 hours per week). In any event, they cannot work before 7:00 A.M. or after 7:00 P.M. (9:00 P.M. in the summer).

The FLSA does not restrict the hours of work for minors who are 16 or 17 years old, but it does prohibit employing them in certain types of hazardous jobs. Some examples are: logging; operating elevators; operating power-driven meat-processing, bakery, or paper-product machinery; wrecking and demolition work; and excavation work.

Some states have passed stricter limitations on child labor than those found in the FLSA. For example, some states have a more extensive list of hazardous jobs and activities, and also limit the number of work hours for all minors under 18, not just for those under 16. Lastly, some states require that employers obtain age certificates to verify the age of employed minors, or require minors to get work permits from school authorities.

LAWS ON UNAUTHORIZED ALIENS

The federal **Immigration Reform and Control Act (IRCA)** prohibits employers from hiring unauthorized alien workers. As part of the hiring process, employers must complete an eligibility form (**Form I9**) for each new employee. The purpose of this form is to ensure that the employer has verified the legal eligibility of the applicant to be employed in this country. The law requires that the form be completed for *all* employees hired, not just for those applicants who "look" foreign. The employer must retain the eligibility form for three years after hiring, or for one year after the employee is terminated, *whichever is later*.

While it is illegal to hire an illegal alien, it is also illegal for employers to discriminate on the basis of national origin or noncitizenship status. The antidiscrimination provisions of IRCA are designed to protect U.S. citizens and "intending citizens" from overly cautious employers who might otherwise simply refuse to hire persons who look or sound foreign.

An "intending citizen" is an alien who has been:

1. lawfully admitted for permanent residence (a green card holder), or
2. granted temporary residence under IRCA's legalization program, or
3. granted asylum under the **Immigration and Nationality Act,** or
4. admitted to the United States as a refugee under IRCA.

The antidiscrimination provisions of IRCA protect aliens in any of these categories *only if* they have filed a declaration of intent to become a citizen. The vast majority of people in categories 2 to 4 eventually become permanent residents, and temporary work authorizations are routinely extended until a green card is issued.

Executive Order 12,989 prohibits federal government contractors from knowingly hiring illegal aliens. Any government contractor found to have knowingly hired illegal aliens can lose its government contracts and be debarred from any future government contracts for a year.

DRUG-TESTING LAWS

U.S. Department of Transportation regulations require preemployment drug testing for truck drivers, and the Federal Aviation Administration has similar regulations covering airline flight personnel. If applicants fail, they can't be hired.

The **Drug-Free Workplace Act** does not require federal contractors to give drug tests to their applicants or employees. This law merely requires contractors to establish a drug-free awareness policy and communicate that policy to their employees.

╱ PROTECTING AGAINST DISCRIMINATION

Laws against discrimination try to ensure that all hiring decisions are made without regard to an applicant's race, color, religion, national origin, sex, age, disability, union affiliation, or veteran status (and in some states the list includes sexual orientation, marital status, and arrest record). Anyone in one or more of these groups is in a **protected category.**

Being in a protected category doesn't guarantee anyone a job. But the law does try to protect the person from employment discrimination based on being in the category. Thus, if an employer decides not to hire an applicant because he is African-American, the employer has violated the law. But, if the employer chooses a white applicant over an African-American applicant because the white candidate has better job skills and more work experience, the employer has not violated the law. The question is whether the reason for the employer's action is based on the applicant's **protected status.** Different treatment based on protected status can be either **intentional** or **adverse-impact discrimination.**

LICENSE TO WORK

Under state laws, special **licenses** are required for certain categories of jobs. An employer trying to hire a lawyer, a teacher, a cosmetologist, or a nurse, for example, must require the applicant to have a specialized license. Without it, he or she can't be hired. In cases such as these, the law is telling employers to set a certain condition for a job.

INTENTIONAL DISCRIMINATION

In a case alleging intentional discrimination, the issue is the employer's motive at the time it made the employment decision. Was the employer motivated by race, sex, religion, national origin, age, or disability, or was the employer motivated by a legitimate nondiscriminatory reason? Trying to discern the motive can involve looking at direct evidence and indirect evidence.

Direct evidence consists of statements made by people who have the authority to make employment decisions. For example, in one case the following comments made by managers regarding a woman under consideration for promotion were found by the court to constitute direct evidence of sex discrimination: the candidate "overcompensated for being a woman"; she should "take a course at charm school"; and she should "walk more femininely, talk more femininely, dress more femininely, wear make-up, have her hair styled, and wear jewelry."

Indirect evidence of discrimination can be found where a member of the protected class applies for a job opening, is qualified for the job but does not get it, and then the employer hires another applicant or continues to seek applicants for the job. This type of evidence raises a presumption of discrimination. However, that presumption can be overcome if the employer can present evidence of a legitimate, nondiscriminatory reason for preferring the nonminority applicant. For example, the employer could show that the other applicant had better references, a better work history, more work experience, or better qualifications than the minority applicant. Unless these reasons are shown to be untrue (e.g., the nonminority did not have better references), no discrimination has occurred. If, however, the employer's reasons are false, there is the possibility that discrimination affected the hiring decision.

ADVERSE IMPACT

Federal law also prohibits conduct that has the effect of discriminating against individuals in a protected class even if the employer's reason for the different treatment is not based on protected status. An example might be an employer who hires only applicants who are at least 5 feet 10 inches tall. On its face, this policy is not based on the protected categories. But the effect of this policy is to disproportionately screen out applicants who are women or are members of certain national origin groups who on the average are shorter than the average white male. This policy, therefore, would have a discriminatory effect, also called **adverse impact.** Adverse-impact discrimination is prohibited unless the employer can prove that the policy is required by business necessity and is significantly related to the job's requirements.

SETTING NONDISCRIMINATORY REQUIREMENTS

Except in cases such as child labor or licenses for certain occupations, the law does not tell the employer what to require in hiring for a job. Rather, the law allows the employer to establish the basic job requirements and work standards—as long as those criteria do not discriminate based on the protected classifications found in federal and state employment discrimination laws.

A job criterion that requires the applicant to be of a specific gender, national origin, religion, or age will almost always violate both federal and state antidiscrimination laws. These laws require employers to consider applicants based on their individual abilities, not on stereotypical assumptions about the group they belong to. Thus, if a factory job entails lifting forty pounds regularly, an employer cannot require that applicants be young men, based on the assumption that men are strong and older people and women are weak. The employer can, however, require that all applicants must be able to regularly lift forty pounds.

"NEUTRAL" JOB REQUIREMENTS

Even job requirements that on their face are neutral can create problems for employers under the discrimination laws. Requiring applicants to pass a written test or possess a college degree can result in disproportionately excluding members of a protected class. For example, many more men than women may be able to pass a mechanical aptitude test. Or in a particular geographic area, many more white than African-American applicants may possess a college de-

---

THE BFOQ EXCEPTION

In a few rare situations, it is an objective fact (not stereotypical assumption) that individuals who are members of a protected class cannot perform the job in question. For example, a filmmaker may require that only men can be hired for male roles. A kosher delicatessen may say that it will hire only Jewish people as butchers. In these examples, sex and religion are **bona fide occupational qualifications (BFOQ)** for the job in question. Both **Title VII** and the **ADEA** allow employers to limit a job to applicants of a specific group if the employer can prove that sex, religion, national origin, or age is a BFOQ for the job. In order for it to qualify as a BFOQ, the employer must prove that there is an objective factual basis for believing that applicants from the excluded group would be unable to safely and efficiently perform the duties of the job. The employer must also prove that the duties involved are so important to the business that the business would be undermined if members of the excluded group were hired.

The BFOQ is a very limited exception to the otherwise general rule that the employer can never specify a particular religion, gender, national origin or age as a criterion for a job. What if customers prefer members of a particular group? That's not enough to justify a BFOQ, nor are stereotypical assumptions about the abilities of a group, or costs associated with hiring members of a particular group. Moreover, race, color, or disability can never qualify as a BFOQ.

---

gree. Such criteria, therefore, would have an adverse impact, excluding individuals who are members of a protected class.

How do you determine whether a neutral requirement results in an adverse impact? You look at a statistical analysis comparing the success rate of the protected group in meeting the requirement with the success rate of the majority group. The touchstone is whether the success rate for the protected group is at least 80 percent of the success rate for the majority group. For example, ten men and ten women take a mechanical aptitude test; eight men and four women pass the test. The success rate for the men is 80 percent and the success rate for the women is 40 percent. Comparison of the success rates for the two groups shows that only 50 percent as many women passed as men; since this is less than 80 percent, the result is that the test has an adverse impact on women.

Does that automatically mean that the employer has discriminated? No. When neutral criteria have an adverse impact, they are considered to violate the employment discrimination laws *unless* the employer can show that the criteria are related to successful performance of the job. Therefore, an employer could justify using a mechanical aptitude test as a qualification for the job of mechanic, but could not justify using it for a clerical position. Similarly, the employer could justify requiring a college degree for a high school teacher but not for an assembly line worker.

Examples of neutral criteria that have been found to have an adverse impact on a protected class include: height and weight standards (exclude women and members of certain ethnic groups); fluency in the English language (excludes members of certain national origin groups); arrest and conviction records (exclude members of certain racial and ethnic groups); and history of garnishment (excludes members of certain racial and ethnic groups). Remember, though, that even if neutral criteria have an adverse impact, an employer can still use them when it can show that the qualification they measure is necessary for successfully performing the job.

SCHEDULING REQUIREMENTS

Besides the qualifications needed to perform the work, most jobs have other kinds of requirements as well, and these too might impact on hiring someone with protected status. Most jobs require employees to be at work during scheduled workdays and working hours. But such requirements may exclude people with certain religious beliefs. Title VII requires employers to **reasonably accommodate** the religious beliefs of applicants and employees unless the accommodation would cause undue hardship on the conduct of the employer's business. This does not mean that an employer cannot establish work schedules and make all applicants and employees abide by such schedules. But it does mean that if an individual cannot comply with a work schedule *because of that individual's religious beliefs,* the employer must try to come up with a reasonable compromise that will meet the employer's business needs and still allow the employee to follow his or her religious beliefs.

The employer is not required to accommodate every employee's whim relating to hours of work. For example, an applicant who does not want to work on Sundays so that he can play golf is not entitled to an accommodation. The applicant who needs time off on Sunday to go to church, however, is entitled to a reasonable accommodation.

Remember, the employer is required to accommodate the employee's religious beliefs only if it does not cause **undue hardship** to the employer's business. If changing the work schedule would cost more money or unduly disrupt the business, the accommodation would be considered to have created an undue hardship. If an accommodation imposes more than *de minimis* (minimal) costs on the employer, it will be considered to create an undue hardship. This is an extremely low standard. For example, in one case spending more than $150 was considered more than *de minimis.* Many work schedule problems, however, can be resolved without any hardship to the employer: another employee may volunteer to swap work schedules, or the religious employee could work longer hours on another day to finish the work left undone.

JOB REQUIREMENTS AND DISABILITIES

Job requirements may also have the effect of screening out an individual based on a disability. The **Americans with Disabilities Act (ADA)** imposes a slightly higher standard on employers to justify a requirement that excludes an individual with a disability. Under the ADA, in order to show that a criterion is related to successful performance of the job in question, an employer must show that the criterion is related to an *essential* function of job performance and not merely

---

WHAT IS ESSENTIAL

The EEOC regulations list several factors to consider in determining the essential functions of a job under the ADA:

1. Does the position exist to perform the function in question? For example, a secretarial position exists to type letters and documents; whereas a receptionist position may exist to greet and direct visitors and answer the phone.
2. Are there a limited number of employees available to perform the function? Even though a receptionist's position does not exist to type, if there is only one secretarial employee at the company and when he is sick or on vacation the receptionist must fill in and perform his duties, then typing may be essential for the receptionist.
3. What is the amount of time spent performing the function? The larger the amount of time devoted to the function, the more likely it is to be essential.
4. What is the effect of not requiring the person to perform the job function in question? For example, a firefighter may be called upon to carry a heavy person from a burning building only rarely (thus spending only a small portion of time performing this duty), yet failure to perform this function could cost a life.
5. What is the work experience of employees who have previously performed this job?

---

an incidental aspect of the job. For example, a job description for a receptionist position requires typing skills. For purposes of Title VII, so long as the receptionist does some typing, the criterion would be considered job-related. Under the ADA, however, the employer would need to show that typing is *essential* to the receptionist's job. If the receptionist spends only 5 percent of the time typing, it is possible that this skill would not be considered essential to the job. Requiring typing skills could have the effect of screening out an individual with only one arm or an individual who is a quadriplegic.

THE BOTTOM LINE

In formulating the criteria for hiring, the employer should remember the words of the Supreme Court, that job qualifications "measure the person for the job and not the person in the abstract." Employers should consider what the essential functions of the job are, and what types of skills are necessary to perform those functions. When the required skills are shown to be directly related to the performance of the job, the criteria will probably pass legal muster.

But quite apart from legal concerns, employers will benefit from thinking hard about what exactly a job is supposed to accomplish, what skills are necessary to get the job done, and what schedule is necessary to do the job. Having determined the skills and qualifications necessary to perform the job, the employer is now in a better position to write up and circulate a job description that will not only meet the requirements of state and federal laws, but also be precisely targeted to the job—and be more likely to result in finding someone to do it well.

GETTING THE WORD OUT

In looking for people to hire, the main idea is to avoid discrimination while at the same time targeting qualified candidates. Advertisements and job descriptions should avoid words suggesting a preferred race, sex, religion, national origin, or age (and in some states sexual orientation and marital status). For example, using the term "recent college graduate" instead of "college degree required" could indicate a preference for young people and discourage older applicants from applying. Using the term "salesman" instead of "salesperson" could suggest that only men should apply.

The method an employer uses to get the word out about job openings can create problems if it has the effect of closing out applicants from a protected class. For example, if the employer's current workforce is predominantly white, and the employer depends on employee word of mouth to circulate news of upcoming job openings, the news will be limited to the employees' acquaintances, who also will be predominantly white people. Members of ethnic and racial minority groups may never hear about the job. Or, to take another example, help-wanted advertisements placed in suburban newspapers and not in the city newspaper are likely to target a mostly white pool of candidates.

Employers can avoid problems by disseminating news of job openings as widely as possible. Placing advertisements in newspapers and magazines with a wide circulation base and using employment agencies or the state job service division can help reach a wide variety of qualified applicants.

APPLICATION FORMS

Many employers require candidates to fill out job application forms. These forms usually ask for information about the applicant's personal, educational and work history. The forms are generally permissible, but federal and state law does affect the type of information that can be requested.

The ADA prohibits an employer from asking any questions relating to the applicant's physical or mental health. Questions that directly seek such information (such as "Do you have a disability?" or "Do you have any health problems?"), as well as questions that indirectly request such information (such as "Have you ever filed a claim for workers' compensation?" or "Do you take any prescription medicines?"), are forbidden.

The NLRA prohibits any questions about union membership or activities. For example, questions such as "Do you belong to a labor organization?" or "Have you ever participated in a strike?" are against the law.

Neither Title VII nor the ADEA prohibits any specific questions. However, the **Equal Employment Opportunities Commission (EEOC)** warns that "inquiries that either directly or indirectly disclose such information (i.e., relating to race, color, religion, national origin, sex or age), unless otherwise explained, may constitute evidence of discrimination prohibited by Title VII." The reason for this caution is that the law prohibits an employer from using information on race, color, religion, national origin, sex or age as the basis for making a hiring decision. If legally the information cannot be used, why would an employer ask about it unless it were for the purpose of taking it into account when making a decision? Only in those rare instances where religion, national origin, sex or age qualifies as a BFOQ should an employer ask questions pertaining to these subjects.

Some state laws, on the other hand, do explicitly restrict allowable questions on application forms. West Virginia, for example, expressly prohibits preemployment questions on race, religion, color, national origin, sex, and age. Wisconsin prohibits questions about an applicant's arrest record. Michigan prohibits questions on race, color, religion, national origin, age, sex, height, weight, marital status, and arrest record. These are just a few examples of the wide variations found in state law.

Employers should review application forms in light of the law of their state. The state constitution, as well as the U.S. Constitution, may limit the type of questions that government employers may ask applicants. These restrictions are discussed in Chapter 7, dealing with public sector employment issues.

HIRING EMPLOYEES

The next step is to actually hire someone. After reviewing the applications and eliminating candidates who do not meet the job qualifications, the employer makes a final selection from among the qualified applicants.

In choosing among many qualified applicants, employers try to figure out which one(s) will be best for the job. They usually rely on personal interviews, reference and background checks and test results. Sometimes employers also take into account affirmative-action considerations. Use of these selection methods must not violate state and federal law.

PERSONAL INTERVIEWS

By their very nature, job interviews are subjective. Employers cannot help but form impressions about an applicant's ambition, motivation, creativity, dependability, and responsibility. Even so, realizing the inherently subjective nature of the process, employers should strive to make an interview as objective (fact-based) as possible. Concentrating on objective information helps avoid decisions made on conscious or subconscious prejudice. It focuses the selection process where it should be—on an individual's qualifications and employment experience. And interviews that focus on job-related issues and relate to legitimate business interests will usually not violate the law.

Employers should also attempt to make job interviews as uniform as possible. The same set of questions should be addressed to all applicants for the same position. This provides a better basis for comparison. It can also prevent the appearance of discrimination. For example, asking only female applicants "Do you plan to get married?" may imply that the employer is rejecting women who plan to marry but not rejecting men for the same reason.

It's in the employer's interest to take careful notes during the interview, to make a written record of the information being used in the hiring decision. Besides being helpful in defending hiring decisions if they're challenged in the future, employers have found that keeping accurate, job-related interview notes improves the quality of the selection process itself.

Obviously, employers should never ask questions in an interview that they are prohibited from asking on a job application form (see discussion on pages 25–26). Interview questions should relate to the job's requirements and the applicant's qualifications, work experience and history. Even when seeking information related to the job, interviewers should be careful to phrase the question so that discrimination is not implied. For example, employers have a legitimate interest in determining the potential employee's commitment to the company and the job. In trying to get this information, however, asking women applicants the following questions is likely to create the suspicion of sex discrimination: "Do you plan to have children?" or "Is your husband's employer likely to transfer him?" A more neutral way to obtain this information is to ask all applicants

---

HANDLING BIASED QUESTIONS

What should you do if an interviewer asks a question that seems out-of-bounds?

You could either swallow hard and answer (and hope the job is worth it), or indicate that the question seems inappropriate (and risk antagonizing the interviewer and losing any chance at the job).

A tactful middle course might be to answer by providing the information the interviewer "really" wants to know. For example, "Oh—you're wondering whether I'll be able to work long hours. I can assure you that I will—my current boss can attest to that."

In any event, you would be well advised to make note of the offending questions as soon as possible after the interview, in case you decide to seek legal advice later on.

---

such questions as "Is there any reason you might not stay with this company for the next few years?" "What are your career objectives?" or "Where do you see yourself in five years?"

CANDIDATES WITH DISABILITIES

Under the ADA, employers can't discriminate against an "individual with a disability who, with or without reasonable accommodation, can perform the essential functions of the employment position." Therefore, in interviewing and making hiring decisions about individuals with disabilities, employers must be careful that their decisions are based on an individual's ability to do the job, not on the person's disability.

If the person can't do the job, the first question is whether the inability to perform its essential function is due to lack of qualifications or the disability. If the employer is hiring for a secretarial position, where the essential function is typing, and the applicant cannot type, then the employer could refuse to hire the candidate even though he or she were blind.

If, however, the blind applicant has typing skills, then the question is whether, with or without a **reasonable accommodation,** he or she can perform the job in question. The applicant may be unable to use the computer keyboard that the employer has at the business, but could use a braille keyboard and do the job. Providing the braille keyboard would be an accommodation that would allow the applicant to perform the essential functions of the job.

What are reasonable accommodations? Generally, they include: making existing facilities readily accessible; restructuring the job; creating part-time or modified work schedules; modifying equipment; or providing readers or interpreters. Some specific examples of accommodations are: providing a deaf employee whose job requires answering the phone with a **telephone device for the deaf (TDD),** or modifying an employee's work hours so he or she can make regularly scheduled appointments for medical treatment. Employers are not required to provide equipment or devices primarily for an individual's personal use, such as corrective glasses, hearing aids or wheelchairs. Whether an employer is required to provide a specific accommodation will depend on whether providing it will cause an undue hardship to the operation of the business.

The ADA defines an **undue hardship** as "an action requiring significant difficulty or expense, when considered in light of the [following] factors":

1. The nature and cost of the accommodation needed;
2. The overall financial resources of the employer's facility, the number of persons employed at that facility, the effect on expenses and resources at the facility, and the impact on the operation of the facility;
3. The financial resources of the employer as a whole, and the overall size of the business; and
4. The type of business that the employer operates, including the composition, structure and function of the workforce and the relationship of the facility in question to the employer as a whole.

Whether or not an accommodation causes an undue hardship is determined case by case. For example, requiring the employer to purchase a TDD may be an undue hardship for a mom-and-pop grocery store, but would not be a hardship for General Motors.

It's generally applicants' responsibility to inform employers of the need for an accommodation; the ADA does not require employers to provide accommodations if they are unaware of the need for any. Also, employers may require applicants to prove they need an accommodation, if the disability is not obvious.

Even if the disability is obvious, employers may not question applicants about the nature or severity of the disability, whether it will interfere with their ability to perform the job or whether they will need treatment or leave time because of the disability. Employers may, however, ask applicants how they would perform the job.

If an applicant with a disability can perform the essential functions of the job with a reasonable accommodation, the ADA prohibits an employer from refusing to hire that person because it would have to provide the accommodation. In other words, if the employer is choosing between two candidates, one of whom has a disability requiring an accommodation, the employer is forbidden from choosing the nondisabled candidate *because it would be cheaper*. The employer can, however, select the nondisabled candidate if he or she is better qualified for the job or as long as the nondisabled candidate was not selected because of the other candidate's disability.

PROTECTING PRIVACY

Employers should also be careful about asking questions that could be seen as an unwarranted intrusion into an individual's personal life. Tort law in some states protects individuals from intentional intrusions into their private affairs in a manner that a reasonable person would find offensive. (**Tort law,** sometimes known as **personal injury law,** is designed to protect people if they or their property are harmed because of someone else's action or failure to act. Many tort cases, such as those arising from automobile collisions, allege negligence, but intentional wrongs, such as invasion of privacy, are also covered.)

Many states have also passed laws that prohibit an employer from discriminating based on an employee's off-duty lifestyle. For example, at least 20 states, including Indiana, South Carolina, and Wyoming, have laws prohibiting employment discrimination based on an employee's off-duty use of tobacco. Other states, such as Wisconsin and Illinois, prohibit employment discrimination based on an employee's off-duty use of any lawful product (which would include not only tobacco but also alcohol).

Last, a few states, such as Colorado and New York, prohibit employment discrimination when an employee engages in any lawful conduct while off-duty. Constitutional protections available to government workers are discussed in Chapter 7.

REFERENCES AND BACKGROUND CHECKS

Requesting references from prior employers is generally not regulated by any federal or state law. However, reference checks that unnecessarily pry into private information or use unreasonable methods to gather data may subject an employer to tort liability for invasion of privacy. So as a rule, background checks should concern only issues relating to performance of the specific job.

Some employers have a credit check done on people they're considering hiring. This raises questions under both Title VII and the Fair Credit Reporting Act. Court cases under Title VII have held that requiring good credit as a condition of employment can result in adverse-impact discrimination, since disproportionately more non-whites than whites live below the poverty line.

The **Fair Credit Reporting Act (FCRA)** is a federal law regulating the use of consumer credit information. An employer using a consumer reporting agency to get information on a prospective employee is subject to FCRA. An employer can get two types of information from a reporting agency—a consumer report and an investigative consumer report. A **consumer report** contains information on the individual's creditworthiness, credit standing, character and general reputation. An **investigative consumer report** contains more detailed and subjective information on a person's character, reputation, and mode of living. Such information is obtained through personal interviews with friends and associates of the consumer.

If an employer decides not to hire someone based in part on information contained in a consumer report, the employer must advise the applicant of that and provide the name and address of the consumer reporting agency that provided the report. Employers intending to get investigative consumer reports on applicants must notify

A DANGER THAT WORKS BOTH WAYS

Background checks also pose a potential danger of defamation suits against employers asked to provide references for employees. (**Defamation** is a tort where the injury is a loss of reputation caused by something untrue that is said or written.) Because of possible liability for defamation, many employers will now only verify that an employee worked for them for a particular period, and not provide an assessment of the employee's performance.

them in writing within three days of requesting a report and inform them of their right to request a complete and accurate disclosure of the nature and scope of the investigation.

Some states, such as Washington and New York, require employers to notify applicants before requesting any type of consumer credit report.

TESTS

Employers sometimes use several types of tests during the selection process: written ability tests; polygraph tests; honesty tests; medical tests; personality tests; drug tests; and AIDS/HIV tests. Each of these tests is regulated in some way by federal or state law, and some are permissible only in certain situations.

However, before we discuss specific tests, there are some considerations that might apply to all tests. Any test given by employers that has the effect of disproportionately excluding members of a protected class creates potential problems under Title VII and the ADA (see discussion on pages 21–23). If a test with an adverse impact is not related to successfully performing the job in question, it violates federal law. Of course, many types of tests have not been shown to have an adverse impact, and their use is not forbidden under the employment discrimination laws.

The second general concern about tests arises under the ADA. When giving tests to applicants with disabilities, employers must ensure that test results reflect the skills that the test is meant to measure and are not affected by an applicant's disability. For example, let's say the employer gives a timed, written test to measure mathematical aptitude. An applicant who is quadriplegic and uses a mechanical device for writing fails the test because he doesn't have sufficient time to complete it. In that instance, the test result was affected by the applicant's disability. If an applicant has a disability impairing his ability to take the test, the employer must modify the way of giving the test so as to accommodate the applicant's disability.

But if the purpose of the test is to measure a skill that is impaired by the disability, the employer is not required to accommodate the applicant. For example, an applicant who is a quadriplegic might fail a speed typing test because his disability prevents him from typing fast. Since the test is designed to measure speed, the employer is not required to modify the test to accommodate the applicant's disability.

Generally, the burden is on applicants taking tests to inform employers of their need for an accommodation.

Besides the above concerns that apply to all employment tests, both federal and state laws regulate specific types of tests.

The **Employee Polygraph Protection Act (EPPA)** applies to almost all private sector employers. Two types of employers are exempted: employers manufacturing or distributing controlled substances, and employers whose primary business is to provide armored car services, security systems, or security personnel. They can give such tests to employees. But the exemption applies only to employees of these companies who either have access to controlled substances or themselves perform the security services. Thus, most clerical and administrative employees who work for drug manufacturers or security companies would be protected under this statute and could not be tested.

Under the terms of the EPPA, employers cannot: request or suggest that applicants undergo lie detector tests; administer lie detector tests to applicants; or refuse to hire an individual because he or she

---

THE LEGAL STATUS OF LIE DETECTOR TESTS

The general rule in American courts is that the results of lie detector tests are not admissible as evidence. The rationale is that the results are not foolproof, and that the give-and-take of examination and cross-examination is a better way of determining the truth.

Of course, being inadmissible as evidence does not keep lie detectors from being used in other situations, and, before the EPPA was passed, about 2 million tests were administered each year by private employers.

has refused to take a lie detector test. The statute defines **lie detector** to include polygraphs, deceptographs, voice stress analyzers, psychological stress evaluators, and any similar mechanical or electrical devices that provide a diagnostic opinion about an individual's honesty.

As defined in the EPPA, federal law forbids only honesty tests that are mechanical or electrical. There are also pen-and-paper honesty tests. While these tests are not covered under the EPPA, a few states regulate them. Both Massachusetts and Rhode Island prohibit employers from giving written as well as mechanical honesty tests. (Using polygraphs to investigate a current workforce is discussed in Chapter 3, in the section on employee discipline.)

The ADA strictly forbids giving **medical tests** to applicants. Such tests may be required, however, after an offer of employment and before the applicant begins working, but only if:

1. all employees for the job in question are required to undergo a medical exam (i.e., particular candidates cannot be singled out for an exam);
2. any information obtained from the exam is maintained in a separate medical file (not made part of the applicant's personnel file) and kept confidential; and
3. the information is not used to discriminate against the employee because of a disability.

As a general rule, **personality tests** that employers use to determine innate intelligence, general personality or psychological characteristics are not regulated. However, if one of these tests provides evidence of a mental disability, it may be considered a medical test, and so be subject to the ADA's strict regulations on medical tests. Also, if such tests have the effect of disproportionately screening out individuals with a mental disability, they would be subject to attack as having an adverse impact under the ADA. The employer would then need to prove that the use of such tests is job-related and a business necessity.

The ADA specifically excludes **drug tests** from its definition of medical examination. Therefore, neither the ADA, nor any other federal law, prohibits employers from requiring applicants to undergo drug tests. However, constitutional guarantees limit the circumstances under which government employers may use drug tests. These limitations on government employers are discussed in Chapter 7.

In addition, several states restrict drug testing in the employment setting. Rhode Island allows drug testing only after an offer of employment has been given (and if the job is conditional on a clean test result). Rhode Island law also says the test sample must be collected in private and positive results must be confirmed. In Minnesota, an employer may not require an applicant to undergo arbitrary or capricious drug testing, and any testing must conform to a written drug testing policy and be conducted by an approved laboratory. North Carolina and Utah allow drug testing so long as certain procedures are followed that provide for reliable testing results.

Finally, the method used by an employer in administering a drug test (such as direct observation of urination) could be considered outrageous and subject the employer to tort liability for invasion of privacy or intentional infliction of emotional distress.

A test to determine the presence of the AIDS/HIV virus is a medical test and as such is subject to ADA restrictions. Moreover, AIDS/HIV is a disability within the meaning of the ADA, and basing an employment decision on the fact that an applicant has AIDS/HIV is prohibited. Many states, moreover, have specific laws that place even further limitations on AIDS/HIV testing. A few states, such as Massachusetts and Florida, prohibit employers from requiring an AIDS/HIV test as a condition of employment. Many more states, like California, Delaware, and Michigan, prohibit an AIDS/HIV test without informed consent and place severe restrictions on the dissemination of test results.

AFFIRMATIVE ACTION

Affirmative-action considerations affect some hiring decisions. This is permissible under federal law as long as it is done according to a valid affirmative-action plan.

An **affirmative-action plan (AAP)** establishes guidelines for recruiting, hiring and promoting women and minorities in order to eliminate the present effects of past employment discrimination. An employer analyzes its current employment practices and the makeup of its workforce for any indications that women and minorities are excluded or disadvantaged. If the employer identifies problems, it devises new policies and practices aimed at solving the problems. The employer then develops goals for measuring progress in correcting the problems and ensuring that women and minorities have equal employment opportunities.

The Supreme Court has held that voluntary private sector AAPs that remedy an obvious racial or gender imbalance in traditionally segregated job categories are lawful. Voluntary AAPs must, however, maintain a balance, trying to assure that minority employees are free from the effect of unlawful discrimination while respecting the employment interests of nonminority employees.

The courts look to several factors in determining the validity of an AAP.

1. The AAP should be designed to eliminate obvious racial or gender-based imbalances in the workforce.
2. The plan cannot "unnecessarily trammel the interests" of nonminority workers. It should not automatically exclude nonminority employees from consideration for the job in question. The minority employee favored by the AAP should be qualified for the job; employers should avoid favoring unqualified workers.
3. The AAP should not adopt strict quotas. It should strive toward realistic goals, taking into account turnover, layoffs, lateral transfers, new job openings, and retirements. These goals should also take into account the number of qualified minorities in the area workforce. Moreover, goals should be temporary, designed to achieve, not maintain, racial and gender balance.
4. Courts are more likely to validate AAPs that focus on recruiting, hiring and promotion practices, rather than plans that give special treatment in the event of a layoff. The courts are more willing to protect a nonminority employee's interests in his current job (as in a layoff situation) than any speculative expectations an applicant might have about a job that he doesn't currently hold (as in hiring and promotion cases).

Neither Title VII, the ADEA, nor the ADA requires AAPs. Employers that have government contracts, however, are often required to develop AAPs. **Executive Order 11,246** requires federal contractors with contracts exceeding $50,000 and a workforce of at least 50 employees to develop AAPs. Many states, such as Iowa and Pennsylvania, require employers that have state contracts to implement AAPs.

Some employers voluntarily adopt AAPs to eliminate the effects of past discrimination and more effectively utilize qualified workers who in the past may have been overlooked because of their race, sex or national origin.

EMPLOYMENT AGENCIES

With the increase in the use of part-timers, temps, and other contingent workers, more and more employers are using employment agencies for recruitment. Employment agencies are chiefly regulated through anti-discrimination laws.

Employment agencies may not discriminate in referring applicants based on any of the protected classifications. The meaning of "discriminate" includes not only intentional discrimination, but also adverse-impact discrimination. An employment agency cannot refuse to refer a worker because he is African-American, even if the company asking for the referral specifically said it wanted only white workers. Moreover, an employment agency using a test to determine which applicants to refer is required to justify the test as related to the job in question if the test disproportionately excludes members of a protected class. Also, in giving any tests, an employment agency should be concerned that the manner of administering the test does not discriminate based on an applicant's disability (see discussion of the ADA's impact on employment tests on pages 33–34).

IRCA also prohibits an employment agency from recruiting or referring illegal aliens, as well as discriminating in recruitment or referral based on national origin or citizenship status.

■

CHAPTER THREE

Terms and Conditions of Employment

Everything from Wages to Sexual Harassment, Leave Time, and Health Insurance

ONCE EMPLOYEES ARE HIRED, their working relationship is governed by the **terms and conditions of employment.** This phrase encompasses all aspects of the working relationship: pay, promotions, vacations, hours of work, training programs, leave time, working environment, discipline and discharge.

Obviously employees care deeply about these terms and conditions, but often they have little or no say in how they are set. They are established by one of three methods: (1) unilateral employer decision; (2) written contract between the employer and the employee (including collective bargaining agreements between a union and employees); and (3) requirements imposed by federal or state law.

WHEN EMPLOYERS DECIDE

Employers decide employment conditions for most workers. They have to follow requirements in the law in some situations but don't have to consult employees in most cases.

Many employers issue handbooks and policy manuals that list the benefits available to employees, as well as the obligations imposed on them. The contents of such manuals are determined by the company, and may be changed and revoked at any time. In some circumstances, however, the benefits that are promised in these handbooks can become binding obligations on the employer.

Most state courts have held that the promises that an employer makes in a personnel manual or handbook may be binding as a **unilateral or implied contract** (as opposed to an explicit written contract signed by both parties that results from negotiation). However, certain requirements must be met.

1. The manual must be circulated to employees. Manuals given only to managers or supervisors for use in dealing with employee problems do not create binding contracts.

2. The language of the manual must contain clear and specific promises of benefits. Vague statements regarding fair treatment do not create a binding obligation. For example, a policy that states, "Any employee who successfully completes his probationary period will receive a 5 percent raise" may be specific enough to be enforceable. However, a policy stating "Employees who successfully complete their probationary period will be considered for a raise" may not create a binding promise to give a raise.

3. Employers can avoid creating a binding promise even if the first two requirements are present, if they clearly and unambiguously inform the employees that the policies contained in a manual or handbook are not meant to create a contract. Such an **express disclaimer** puts the employees on notice that they cannot rely on the policies as a statement of terms and conditions of employment.

Even when a handbook or manual creates a contract, the employer is generally free to revoke or revise it at any time. Once the employer gives notice to employees that a policy has been changed, the old policy is no longer enforceable for situations arising after the change. If an employer changed its policy from a specific promise of a 5 percent raise upon completion of a probationary period to merely a statement that a raise would be considered, employees who complete their probationary period after the notice of change would not be able to claim a right to a raise. However, an employee who completed the probationary period before the change was made may be able to successfully claim the raise.

WRITTEN EMPLOYMENT CONTRACTS

Few employees have individual written employment contracts. Such contracts tend to be limited to high-level executives, sports stars, actors, and other highly skilled professional workers. When such a contract exists, however, both the employer and employee are bound by it. Failure to live up to its terms is a breach of contract, and the breaching party is liable under state contract law.

One other group of employees has employment conditions regulated by written contract—employees who are represented by a labor union that has negotiated a collective bargaining agreement with their employer. The effect and enforceability of such contracts will be discussed in Chapter 6, dealing with unions in the workplace.

THE LAW'S IMPACT

Before discussing some specific laws, let's look at an important general consideration. Under the antidiscrimination laws, members of a protected class can't be singled out by special or different terms and conditions of employment. The terms and conditions must apply uniformly. Even if the law does not require the employer to provide a benefit (for example, vacation time), if the employer decides to provide the benefit it must be available to all employees without regard to race, color, religion, national origin, sex, age, disability, or other protected status.

That means an employer could not give pay raises to all the men but not to the women. It could, however, give raises to all the assembly workers but not to the office workers. In the first example the reason for the difference in treatment was membership in a protected class (sex). In the second, the reason for the difference in treatment was a difference in job duties.

While many aspects of the working relationship are left to the employer's discretion, federal and state law does establish a minimum level of benefits for some terms and conditions of employment.

MINIMUM WAGE LAWS

The **Fair Labor Standards Act (FLSA)** requires employers to pay a minimum of $4.75 per hour. As of September 1, 1997, employers will be required to pay a minimum of $5.15 an hour. A few employers are not covered by the FLSA, but almost every state has passed minimum wage laws for employers doing business in the state. Most states peg their minimum wage at the same level as the FLSA. About seven states have a lower minimum and about nine states a higher one. In states that have set their minimum higher than federal law, the higher state wage applies to *all* employers doing business in that state, even if that employer is covered under the FLSA. For example, all employers doing business in Hawaii must pay their workers a minimum of $5.25 an hour. However, if the state minimum is lower than the FLSA, employers covered under the FLSA have to pay the FLSA rate; only employers not covered by the FLSA can pay the lower state wage rate.

The minimum wage must be paid for every hour worked in any

YOUTH SUBMINIMUM WAGE

Employees under 20 years of age may be paid a subminimum wage of $4.25 an hour during their first 90 consecutive calendar days of employment. After the first 90 days, however, the regular minimum wage must be paid. Moreover, an employer is prohibited from discharging or reducing the hours of employees who are paid the regular minimum wage in order to hire youths at the subminimum rate.

---

workweek; an employee who works for 20 hours must be paid a minimum of $95 ($103 after September 1, 1997). **Hours worked** generally include all the time spent by employees performing their job duties during the workday. When an employee's job requires travel during the workday, such as a service technician who repairs furnaces at customers' homes, the time spent traveling is considered hours worked for which the employee must receive compensation. Hours worked also includes preparatory time spent before the start of the workday, if the time is required to perform the job. For example, workers who have to sharpen their knives at a meat-processing plant, or workers required to wear special protective clothing at a chemical plant, must be compensated for this preparatory time. Mandatory attendance at lectures, meetings and training programs is considered hours worked, as are rest periods and coffee breaks shorter than 20 minutes.

THE COIN OF THE REALM

The minimum wage must usually be paid in money, but the employer can take a credit for the cost of providing certain noncash benefits to employees. An employer can credit the reasonable cost of meals, lodging and other facilities customarily provided to employees. An example is lodging provided to a "house mother" who lives in a residential rehabilitation facility.

To credit the cost of such noncash benefits, they must be furnished for the employee's convenience and they must be voluntarily accepted by the employee. Examples of noncash items whose fair value can be credited against the minimum wage are: meals furnished at the company cafeteria, housing furnished by the company for residential purposes, and fuel or electricity used by the employee for nonbusiness purposes.

For the purpose of minimum wage laws, employers can't take a credit for employee discounts and money employees are required to pay for breakage or cash shortages.

What is *not* considered hours worked for purposes of the minimum wage? Examples include commuting time to work; lunch or dinner breaks of at least 30 minutes; changing clothes when done for the benefit of the employee; and on-call time away from the employer's premises that the employee can use for his or her own purposes. In determining whether workers should be paid for on-call time, courts look at how much control the employer has over the employee during that time, and whether the employee is free to use the time as he or she wishes. If an employee is prevented from doing only a limited number of things while on-call (such as consuming alcohol), then the worker does not have to be paid.

Employers are allowed to credit tips against the minimum wage for employees in jobs that customarily receive more than $30 a month in tips (for example, a waiter or beautician). Regardless of how much an employee earns in tips, the employer must pay at least $2.13 per hour in cash to the employee. If a waiter works 40 hours in a week during which he earns $200 in tips (which is $5.00 per hour in tips) the employer would still have to pay the waiter $2.13 per hour, even though the employee's tips place his wage rate above $4.75 per hour.

Of course, the employer is allowed to credit only the amount the employee actually receives in tips. The employee must always receive *at least* the minimum wage when wages and tips are combined.

For example, a waitress works 40 hours in a week and earns a total of $80 in tips, which is $2 per hour. The employer is allowed to take $2 per hour as credit against the $4.75 minimum wage and thus is required to pay the waitress at least $110 for that week's work ($4.75 minus $2.00 tip credit equals $2.75 per hour for 40 hours). Suppose that same waitress works 40 hours a week and earns a total of $120 in tips, which is $3 per hour. The employer would still be required to pay $2.13 per hour, even though the combined amount of tips and wages exceeds $4.75 minimum wage, because the law requires the employer to pay no less than $2.13 per hour to its tipped employees.

Employers may not take the tip credit unless they inform their employees about it. Employers must also be able to prove that the employee actually receives tips equal to the tip credit taken by the employer.

OTHER WAGE LAWS

Employers performing work under certain types of federal government contracts are covered by a series of wage laws dealing with government contractors. A federal contractor manufacturing or furnishing to the government materials, supplies, articles, or equipment in excess of $10,000 is covered by the **Walsh-Healey Act.** This law requires that all employees receive the prevailing minimum rate for similar work performed in the locality. The prevailing minimum rate is determined by the secretary of labor.

The **Davis-Bacon Act** requires contractors performing work valued in excess of $2,000 on federal construction projects to pay their employees the prevailing area wage and fringe benefit rate, which is determined by the secretary of labor. The **Service Contract Act** requires that all employees performing service work (such as guards, janitors, and maintenance employees) under contract to the federal government be paid the federal minimum wage. If the value of the contract exceeds $2,500, then the employees must also be paid the prevailing area wage and fringe benefit rate as determined by the secretary of labor.

OVERTIME

The **FLSA** and comparable state laws also regulate wage rates for overtime work. If employees work more than 40 hours during any workweek, employers must pay them 1½ times their regular rate of pay. The overtime rate applies to each hour, or fraction of an hour, worked over 40 in any workweek.

In computing overtime pay, the employer must use the employee's regular rate of pay, not the minimum wage rate. When an employee is paid by the hour, the regular rate and the hourly rate are the same. For example, an employee who is paid $6.00 an hour and works 43 hours in one week is owed $27 in overtime pay. The overtime rate is $9 per hour ($6 per hour times $1^1/_2$), and the hours worked in excess of 40 is 3. The employee's salary for that week would be $240 ($6 per hour for 40 hours) plus the overtime pay of $27 ($9 per hour for 3 hours) for a total of $267.

When an employee is paid a salary or commission, the employee's pay must be converted to an hourly rate to compute overtime. You get the hourly rate by dividing the employee's pay for the week by the number of hours worked in that week. Let's take the example of an employee who is paid $225 a week as a standard salary for any week, including one of 40 hours. One week the employee works 45 hours. That makes the employee's regular hourly rate for that week $5 per hour ($225 divided by 45). The employer owes the employee an additional $37.50 for the 5 hours of overtime worked in that week. The overtime rate is $7.50 ($5 per hour times $1^1/_2$), and the hours worked in excess of 40 is 5. The employee's salary for that week would be $225 plus the overtime pay of $37.50 ($7.50 per hour for 5 hours) for a total of $262.50.

Not all employers are covered by the FLSA, and even among those that are, certain categories of employees are exempt from its provisions: salespeople, computer professionals, executive employees, professional employees, and administrative employees.

Retail commission salespeople must be paid at least the minimum

---

WHEN DO YOU GET OVERTIME?

Do you get overtime for working a tough 12-hour day? Not necessarily. Overtime is figured on a work*week*, not a work*day*. Overtime is based solely on time worked (regardless of what day) in excess of 40 hours in a workweek. Work on Saturday, Sunday, or a holiday does not automatically entitle you to overtime pay; it depends on whether you have already worked 40 hours for that week.

---

wage but are exempt from the overtime requirements if certain conditions are met. First, the regular rate of pay for the salesperson must be in excess of $1^1/_2$ times the federal minimum wage (i.e., the regular rate of pay must be in excess of $7.13 per hour or $7.73 after September 1, 1997). Second, more than half of the salesperson's pay must come from commissions on goods or services.

Outside salespeople are exempt from both the minimum wage and overtime requirements if they meet three qualifications:

1. The individual is employed to make sales or to obtain orders or contracts for services.
2. The employee customarily and regularly spends time performing such sales work away from the employer's place of business.
3. The amount of time spent performing nonsales work cannot exceed 20 percent of the hours worked by that employer's nonexempt employees (i.e., those employees who must be paid the minimum wage and overtime). Work that is incidental to sales activity (such as writing sales reports or attending sales conferences) is considered sales work.

Computer professionals who are paid at least $27.63 an hour are exempt from the overtime requirements if certain conditions are met. The definition of a computer professional is an employee who works as a "computer systems analyst, computer programmer, software engineer, or other similarly skilled worker." Employees in this category are exempt if their primary work duties fall into one of the following categories:

1. the applications of systems analysis techniques and procedures, including consulting with users, to determine hardware, software or system functional specifications;
2. the design, development, documentation, analysis, creation, testing or modification of computer systems or programs;
3. the design, documentation, testing, creation or modification of computer programs related to machine operating systems;
4. a combination of the duties described in the preceding three categories, the performance of which requires the same level of skill.

Executive employees who are paid at least $155 a week are exempt from both the minimum wage and overtime requirements. A five-part test is used to determine if an employee is an executive. First, the employee must be engaged in some form of management work. In determining the extent of management responsibility, the following factors are considered: the importance of the managerial duties as compared to other job responsibilities; the exercise of discretionary authority; relative freedom from supervision; and a salary that is relatively more than workers performing nonmanagerial duties. Second, the employee must customarily direct the work of two or more employees. Third, the employee has the authority to hire, fire or make recommendations concerning the employment and discipline of other workers. Fourth, the employee regularly exercises discretionary powers. Last, the employee does not spend more than 20 percent of his or her time on activity not related to the executive duties of the job.

An executive employee whose salary is greater than $250 a week need meet only two requirements in order to be exempt from the FLSA. First, the employee's primary duty must be to manage the enterprise or a recognized department within the enterprise. Second, the employee's primary duties must include the direction of two or more employees.

Professional employees with a weekly salary of at least $170 are exempt from both the minimum wage and overtime provision if they meet certain requirements. First, the employee's primary work must require specialized study, or the employee is a teacher in an educational institution. Second, the work must be of a predominantly intellectual character and nonroutine, requiring the consistent exercise of discretion and judgment. Third, the employee does not spend more than 20 percent of his or her time on nonprofessional work.

Professional employees who earn at least $250 a week, meet the first requirement listed above, and consistently exercise discretion and judgment are also exempt.

Administrative employees with a weekly salary of at least $155 are also exempt from both the minimum wage and overtime provisions if certain requirements are met. First, the employee's primary work must not be manual but must be office work directly related to management policies or general business operations. Second, the employee must customarily exercise discretion and independent judgment. Third, the employee must perform one of the following jobs: regularly assisting an executive or administrator; performing special assignments under general supervision; performing specialized or technical work that requires some special training and is only generally supervised. Last, the employee must not spend more than 20 percent of his or her time on nonadministrative work.

Administrative employees who earn more than $250 a week need meet only two requirements in order to be exempt. First, the employee's primary duty must be office work directly related to management policies. Second, the employee's work must require the exercise of independent judgment.

SETTING WAGE RATES

Assuming the wage requirements of the FLSA and state law are met, an employer can use its discretion in setting wage rates for jobs *as long as it does not base pay differentials on membership in a protected class* (i.e., race, gender, age, etc). Pay differentials based on protected status violate state and federal antidiscrimination laws. In

---

MAKING A RECORD

The FLSA requires employers to maintain and preserve certain wage records to verify their compliance with the law. Employee payroll records must be retained for three years, and must contain such information as employee names, hours worked each workday and workweek, wages paid, deductions from wages, straight-time wages and overtime paid. The employer must also maintain for two years documentation in support of its payroll records, such as time cards, work schedules, and order and billing records.

---

addition, the **Equal Pay Act (EPA)** specifically prohibits employers from paying different wages to employees of either sex for work that requires substantially equal skill, effort and responsibility and is performed under similar working conditions. However, an employer may set different wage rates based on seniority, skill, merit, quality, or differences in job content.

EPA requirements apply to jobs that are substantially equal. For example, let's say a beauty salon hires a male barber and a female beautician. The barber cuts the hair of male clients, and the beautician cuts the hair of female clients. The beauty salon pays the barber $2.50 per hour more than it pays the beautician. These two employees are performing substantially equal jobs: the skill of cutting hair is the same, the effort used is the same, the responsibility the two employees have for cutting hair is the same, and they work under similar working conditions since they both work in the same beauty salon. In this case the employer has violated the EPA. If, however, the barber has five years' experience cutting hair, and the beautician has only two years' experience, the employer could justify the difference in wage rate as based on seniority and not sex.

"COMPARABLE WORTH" REMAINS A THEORY

The EPA applies when jobs are the same. It does not apply, however, where jobs are different but their worth to the employer is similar.

Some scholars think it should apply to jobs of similar value. This is the **comparable worth** theory. Under it, if the largely female office staff of a trucking company is as valuable to the company as its largely male drivers, the two groups should be paid the same.

The practical problem is that it is very difficult—if not impossible—to prove that workers who do different work are equally valuable. Under the law as it stands now, if workers do different kinds of jobs, that difference justifies paying them at different rates.

WAGE PAYMENTS AND GARNISHMENTS

While federal law does not specify when wages must be paid, virtually every state has a wage payment law dealing with time for payment, deductions from wages, and garnishment. State law generally requires that employees be paid weekly, semimonthly or monthly.

Employers are *required* to deduct taxes and certain amounts that have been garnished from an employee's paycheck. They are *allowed* to deduct certain items from an employee's paycheck if the employee has authorized the deduction. Examples of allowable deductions are: union dues, charitable contributions, and insurance premiums. These deductions are allowed even if the amount received by the employee after the deduction falls below the minimum wage.

Other items cannot be deducted from paychecks if the deduction would cause the pay to fall below the minimum wage. Examples of such items are: cost of work uniforms, cost of cleaning work uniforms, employee breakage, and cash shortage debts.

Most states prohibit certain deductions from pay regardless of the circumstances. For example, California prohibits deductions for the cost of a required preemployment physical exam; Connecticut prohibits any deductions without written authorization from the employee; and Hawaii prohibits any deductions for replacement costs due to employee breakage.

Both the federal **Consumer Credit Protection Act** and state laws limit the amount that can be garnished from a worker's paycheck. A **garnishment** is a court order requiring that earnings be withheld from a worker's paycheck and paid to a person or business to whom the worker owes a debt. The federal law limits the maximum amount that can be garnished to the lesser of 25 percent of an employee's take-home pay or that part of take-home pay that exceeds 30 times the federal minimum wage.

For example, an employee's take-home pay is $400 a week. Currently, 30 times the federal minimum wage is $142.50; this worker's wage exceeds that amount by $257.50. But this excess amount is subject to garnishment only if it is less than 25 percent of the worker's wage. Since 25 percent of this worker's wage is $100, the maximum amount that can be garnished is $100. If, on the other hand, the employee's weekly take-home pay was $150, his wages would exceed 30 times the minimum wage by $7.50, whereas 25 percent of his wages would be $37.50. The maximum amount that could be garnished in this case is $7.50, which is the lesser of the two figures.

The law permits a larger amount to be deducted if the debt is owed for child-support payments, Chapter 13 bankruptcy or back taxes. Federal law also prohibits an employer from discharging an employee because his or her wages have been garnished once.

Most state garnishment laws contain the same limitations. However, some states limit garnishment more, in which case the employer must comply with state law. For example, Alaska limits the amount that can be garnished to the amount by which the employee's weekly net pay exceeds $350, and Delaware limits the amount to 15 percent of the employee's wages.

HOURS

Besides the FLSA, several federal laws impact upon the hours of certain workers. For example, federal laws regulate the hours of people working in interstate transportation. The **Hours of Service Act** limits the working hours of railroad employees engaged in train operations. Train employees must be given 8 consecutive hours off during a 24-hour period, and cannot work more than 12 consecutive hours at any one time. A crew member who has worked the 12-hour maximum must be given 10 hours off before returning to work.

U.S. Department of Transportation regulations limit the hours of truck drivers working for employers regulated under the **Motor Carriers Act** (which generally covers interstate and commercial motor vehicle transportation companies). As a rule, drivers cannot drive for more than 10 hours following 8 consecutive off-duty hours, and cannot drive at all if they have been on duty (whether driving or not) for 15 hours following 8 consecutive off-duty hours.

The **Federal Aviation Administration** has regulations limiting the hours of airline crew members. The limitations vary depending on the type of airline operation (overseas, domestic, nonpassenger, etc.). For example, flight crews who work on domestic and commuter passenger airlines cannot work more than 1,000 hours a year, 100 hours a month, or 30 hours in any seven consecutive days. Also, such crew members must be given scheduled rest periods of at least 11 consecutive hours for 9 or more hours of scheduled flight time.

Outside the transportation industry, employers are generally free to set the work schedule. Some state laws and regulations, however, require employers to give employees certain rest and meal periods during the course of a workday. Connecticut and Delaware require employers to give 30-minute unpaid meal breaks to employees who work at least 7½ consecutive hours. Maine requires employers to provide 30 consecutive minutes of rest time (which may be used for meals) to employees who work more than 6 consecutive hours. Minnesota requires employers to give reasonable bathroom break time every 4 hours.

LEAVE TIME

Contrary to popular belief, no law makes an employer give employees paid vacation time or paid holidays. This issue is left to the discretion of the employer.

However, several federal laws mandate leave time under certain situations. The **Family and Medical Leave Act (FMLA)** requires employers to grant eligible employees up to 12 weeks of unpaid leave with right of reinstatement to the job. Employees are eligible for leave if they have worked at least 1,250 hours for their employer for at least one year, and if there are at least 50 employees at their work site or at least 50 employees within 75 miles of their work site.

Leave under the FMLA is available only for the following reasons:

1. because of the birth of a child and in order to care for the child;
2. because of adoption or foster-care placement of a child;
3. because of a serious health condition that makes the employee unable to perform his duties; or

4. in order for the employee to care for a spouse, child or parent with a serious medical condition.

Leave time is limited to 12 weeks of unpaid leave during any 12-month period. The 12 weeks of leave do not necessarily have to be taken all at once. Under certain circumstances an employee is eligible for intermittent leave or leave on a reduced schedule. Generally, the 12 weeks must be taken consecutively when the leave is for the birth, adoption or placement of a child, but if the leave is for either the employee's or a relative's serious medical condition, intermittent leave or a reduced schedule is available.

The FMLA regulations define a **serious medical condition** as a physical or mental illness, injury or impairment that involves one of the following: (1) any period of incapacity or treatment in connection with inpatient care at a health care institution; (2) a period of incapacity requiring absence from work, school or daily activity in excess of three days that also requires continuing treatment by a health care provider; or (3) continuing treatment by a health care provider for a chronic or long-term health condition that is either incurable or so serious that, if not treated, it would result in a period of incapacity in excess of three days.

The FMLA does not require employers to pay employees during their leave period. Employers can pay employees, or advance vacation pay, but they don't have to. The law does say, however, that if

---

LETTING YOUR EMPLOYER KNOW

You have to provide at least 30 days' advance notice to your employer before taking family leave, if such notice is practicable. If 30 days' notice is not possible because of unforeseen or emergency circumstances, you must notify your employer as soon as possible. Your employer may require you to provide medical certification when leave is requested for your own, or a relative's, serious medical condition.

---

employers provide health insurance coverage they must continue that coverage during the leave with no additional charge to employees. At the end of the leave period, employers must reinstate employees to their previous position or an equivalent position.

State laws also require leave for family and medical reasons. These laws are important for two reasons. Some of the laws regulate employers that are not subject to the FMLA; for example, Oregon's law applies to employers with 25 or more employees. Second, some states may grant more generous leave time to employees. For example, North Dakota's law grants up to four months of leave, though it applies only to state government employers.

Under **Title VII,** an employer must treat time off from work due to pregnancy the same as it treats time off for any other medical condition. Therefore, if an employer's policy provides for paid sick leave, it must be available to employees who are absent due to pregnancy. If an employer reinstates a worker who is absent from work because of surgery or mononucleosis, the employer must reinstate a worker after childbirth.

Title VII also requires an employer to reasonably accommodate the religious practices of its employees. An employee who needs time off from work to attend a religious convention, or who cannot work on Saturday because it is the Sabbath, may be entitled to leave time or a modification of work schedule. The question is whether the modification or time off will create an undue hardship on the employer's business.(See discussion on page 22.)

Under the **ADA,** an employer may be required to give an employee with a disability leave time as a reasonable accommodation. The ADA lists both flexible leave policies and modified work schedules as examples of possible reasonable accommodations for employees with a disability. Once again, there is an exception if these practices would cause undue hardship on the employer's business. What might be a reasonable accommodation? The employer may be required to modify the work schedule of an employee with a mental disability to enable him or her to attend psychiatric sessions during the workday. Or an employer may be required to grant an employee unpaid leave time to undergo medical treatment related to a disability.

The **Uniformed Services Employment and Reemployment Rights Act (USERRA)** requires employers to grant an unpaid leave of absence of up to five years to any employee serving in the "uniformed services." The **uniformed services** include the full-time and reserve components of the Army, Navy, Marine Corps, Air Force, Coast Guard, and National Guard and the commissioned corps of the Public Health Service.

Upon honorable discharge, employees are entitled to reinstatement to their former position, with the same seniority and other rights and benefits that they had on the date they began uniformed service. They are also entitled to additional seniority-based rights and benefits they would have attained had they remained continuously employed. While in uniformed service, they are to be treated as if on leave of absence, and are entitled to any non-seniority-based benefits that are available generally to employees on leave of absence.

The **Jury System Improvements Act** is a federal law that prohibits an employer from disciplining or discharging an employee because he or she has been called to serve on a federal jury. Additionally, about 37 states have laws prohibiting employers from firing workers called to perform jury service in the state court system. In effect, these laws require employers to grant unpaid leave to employees performing jury service and reinstate employees to their jobs when jury service is over.

Though there is no federal law in this area, about 30 states, including New York, Ohio and Maryland, have laws making employers give employees time off to vote in elections. These laws try to ensure that employees aren't prevented from voting by the need to be at work. The key is when the polls are open and when employees are required to be at work. If an employee's work shift is from three in the afternoon until eleven at night, the employer would not have to give the employee time off to vote. Polls in every state are open early in the day. But if the employee works from 8:00 A.M. until 6:00 P.M., the employer may be required to grant time off. Most of the laws apply to all elections, whether federal, state or local, although a few are limited to particular types of elections. Most do not allow the employer to deduct wages for the time off.

HARASSMENT

The law does not protect employees from many kinds of harassment. Naturally, personality clashes, abusive supervisors, and coworkers who don't get along create problems, but they're often ones without legal remedies. Under certain circumstances, however, the anti-discrimination laws come into play.

Title VII's prohibition against discrimination includes harassment in the workplace aimed at workers because of their race, religion, sex or national origin. There are two types of discriminatory harassment: creation of a hostile work environment, and quid pro quo harassment.

Hostile environment harassment involves denigrating individuals based on their race, religion, gender or national origin, and creating an intimidating, hostile or offensive working environment. It can consist of unwelcome verbal or physical conduct. A single isolated incident or comment will generally not be considered sufficient to create a hostile environment unless the conduct is extremely outrageous and egregious. Examples of hostile environment harassment are: vulgar or lewd comments about women; obscene or sexually suggestive posters; off-color or "ethnic" jokes; offensive racial or ethnic comments. The issue is whether the comments and conduct are severe enough to create a work environment that a reasonable person would find hostile or abusive.

Such comments and conduct must also be unwelcome to the victim or target of the harassment, in the sense that the victim did not "invite" the comments or conduct. The fact that a worker tolerates racial or sexual remarks or attempts to laugh them off in order to fit in with the other workers does not mean that the conduct is welcome or invited.

Supervisors, managers, coworkers, and even customers can be

responsible for creating a hostile environment. An employer can be held liable for the actions of its own employees as well as its customers when their conduct creates a hostile environment. However, companies have defenses against liability. The key is to have a policy against harassment with an effective enforcement mechanism (see box). The EEOC has taken the position that a company that has an effective harassment policy will not be liable for supervisor/manager conduct creating a hostile environment unless it was aware of the problem and did not take appropriate action to stop the harassment.

When coworkers or customers create a hostile environment, a company will not be liable unless it had knowledge or had reason to know that the harassment occurred and failed to take the proper corrective actions.

The second type of harassment occurs only in relation to sex discrimination. It is known as quid pro quo harassment. The EEOC has

---

PREVENTING HARASSMENT

Employers can take several steps to prevent harassment in the workplace. They can

1. develop a written policy dealing with discriminatory harassment, indicating that it is against the law and violates company policy;
2. provide an effective complaint mechanism for workers who have been subjected to harassment, including a way for employees to bypass their supervisor when the supervisor participates in the harassment or fails to address a complaint;
3. promptly undertake a complete and confidential investigation as soon as they are made aware of a problem and impose appropriate disciplinary action if the complaint has merit; and
4. prevent sexual harassment before it occurs by circulating or posting the company anti-harassment policy and the EEOC guidelines on sexual harassment; they can also express strong disapproval of such conduct and tell employees of their right to be free from harassment.

---

defined **quid pro quo harassment** as "unwelcome sexual advances, requests for sexual favors, and other verbal or physical conduct of a sexual nature . . . when . . . submission to or rejection of such conduct is used as the basis for employment decisions." When a job benefit is directly tied to submitting to unwelcome sexual advances, the employee is a victim of quid pro quo harassment. An example would be a supervisor promising an employee a raise if she will go out on a date with him, or telling an employee she will be fired if she doesn't have sex with him.

Such sexual conduct is prohibited whenever it is **unwelcome.** If an employee shows by her conduct that sexual advances are unwelcome, it does not matter that she eventually "voluntarily" succumbs to the harassment. Her actions are the result of coercion—fear of the employment consequences if she continues to reject the advances. In deciding whether sexual advances are unwelcome, courts will often allow evidence concerning the employee's dress, behavior, and language, as well as other indications of whether she welcomed the advances.

Only a person with supervisory or managerial authority can engage in quid pro quo harassment, since it requires the harasser to have the authority to grant or withhold job benefits. In general, an employer is **strictly liable** when a supervisor engages in quid pro quo harassment. This means that even if the employer has no knowledge

---

IF YOU'RE A VICTIM OF SEXUAL HARASSMENT

If you've been subjected to sexual harassment, immediately notify your supervisor. If the supervisor is the harasser, go to the supervisor's superiors. Employers cannot solve the problem if they do not know about it.

If there is a grievance procedure, you should use it. You can also express your disapproval of the conduct to the perpetrator, and tell him or her to stop.

You should keep a written record of all incidents of harassment, detailing the place, time, persons involved, and any witnesses.

---

of the supervisor's conduct and has a policy forbidding harassment, the employer is still responsible for the supervisor's quid pro quo harassment.

It is clear that unwelcome sexual remarks or advances by men directed at women are prohibited. So are unwelcome remarks and advances made by women to men. But courts disagree about whether same-sex harassment is prohibited. Many courts have held that it is. One court wrote, "when a supervisor sexually harasses a subordinate because of the subordinate's sex, that supervisor 'discriminate[s]' on the basis of sex." In that analysis, the issue is whether the sexual comments or advances are unwelcome, not whether the employees involved are the same gender or different genders. Other courts, however, have held that since same-sex harassment involves individuals of the same gender, there is no discrimination "on the basis of sex," and have found that such conduct is not prohibited.

Given the unsettled state of the law, to say nothing of the fact that harassment certainly interferes with efficiency and productivity in the workplace, employers would be well advised to prohibit *any* type of sexual harassment, regardless of the gender of the individuals involved.

PERSONNEL FILES

Federal and state laws deal with both the confidentiality of personnel files and employees' access to personnel files.

The **ADA** requires employers to keep any employee medical records confidential and separate from personnel files. The law states that the only persons who may be informed about an employee's medical conditions are first aid or safety personnel if the medical condition may require emergency treatment, and government officials investigating compliance with the ADA. The employer may also inform supervisors and managers about restrictions on work duties or necessary accommodations required by a disability.

The **Privacy Act** forbids federal government employers from disclosing any information contained in an employee's files without his or her written consent. The Privacy Act gives federal government workers access to their personnel records and permits them to make a copy of any portion of the documents. It also gives them a procedure to challenge the information contained in their files. Many states have similar laws regulating access to the files of state public employees.

Some states also protect certain information about private sector employees. For example, California, Florida and Pennsylvania prohibit disclosure of employee medical records. At least one state, Connecticut, prohibits disclosure of any employee personnel information without the written consent of the employee in question. Moreover, unnecessary disclosure of information that the employee reasonably expects will be kept private can make an employer liable under state tort law for invasion of privacy or intentional infliction of emotional distress.

The **Occupational Safety and Health Act (OSH Act)** requires private sector employers to give employees access to medical records that they must maintain when employees are exposed to potentially toxic materials at work. The **National Labor Relations Act (NLRA)** requires private sector employers to give unions information that is necessary and relevant for collective bargaining purposes. This can include access to employee personnel files. There is, however, no duty to disclose such information directly to the employee.

About 15 states, including California, Massachusetts, Michigan and Wisconsin, grant employees access to their personnel files. Some of these laws also provide procedures enabling employees to challenge information in their files.

OTHER LAWS

• **Drug testing.** Employers sometimes require employees to undergo drug tests. These can either be random or based on suspicion of drug use by certain employees. Generally, the same rules that apply to drug testing in the preemployment phase (discussed in Chapter 2), apply to drug tests for current employees. Of course, in a unionized workplace the employer would have to bargain with the union before implementing drug tests for current employees.

• **Restricting smoking at work.** Generally, an employer is free to restrict smoking at work, though in a unionized workplace the employer would be required to bargain with the union before implementing such a policy. Indeed, many state laws *require* employers to establish no-smoking policies for certain work areas, such as hospitals and restaurants. At the same time, about 20 states prohibit employers from discriminating against employees because they use tobacco off-duty, away from the workplace.

• **English-only rules.** Employers restricting their employees' ability to speak any language but English on the job may run afoul of **Title VII.** An English-only rule could have an adverse impact on persons of certain ethnic or national origins, though it could be justified if the employer can show that it is job-related and consistent with business necessity. For example, a rule may be allowable if it requires employees to speak English when dealing with customers, but could be discriminatory if it required English during break and lunch times.

• **Dress codes.** Dress and grooming policies are generally allowed, but occasionally they can run afoul of **Title VII.** Some employers, for example, impose a dress code on female employees but not on male employees. This could violate Title VII's prohibition against different treatment based on sex. Or a grooming code may impact more severely on a particular protected class, thus having an adverse impact under Title VII. For example, a rule requiring employees to be clean-shaven may adversely impact members of certain religious groups. In that case, the employer would have to show a business necessity to enforce the policy.

Enforcement of a dress code may, in some circumstances, violate the **NLRA.** See discussion concerning union insignia in Chapter 6.

• **Right to privacy at work.** Employers sometimes attempt to monitor employees' performance through either listening in on their telephone calls or using video cameras to monitor them at work.

Sometimes employers search workers or their property, usually to combat theft. The law imposes few limitations on such practices.

Title III of the Omnibus Crime Control and Safe Streets Act is a federal law prohibiting eavesdropping on, or wiretapping, phone calls. There are two exceptions, however. One allows an employer to listen in on an extension telephone used in the ordinary course of business. A second exception allows the employer to monitor calls if employees have been expressly notified that their telephone conversations will be monitored. Some courts have indicated, however, that once the private nature of a telephone conversation is determined, any continued eavesdropping by the employer would not be in the ordinary course of business and may subject the employer to liability. Most state laws relating to telephone monitoring are modeled after this federal statute.

A few states have more stringent requirements for monitoring employees' phone calls. For example, California requires an audible beep on the line to alert the caller that the conversation is being monitored. Other states, such as Pennsylvania, prohibit eavesdropping without the consent of both parties to the conversation. A few states, however, such as Georgia, specifically allow employers to monitor telephone calls to improve business service.

The **NLRA** prohibits employer surveillance of union activity, discussions about unions, and union meetings. Thus, any monitoring of employees that has the effect of closely observing union conduct violates the law.

Some state laws also regulate employers monitoring workers. Connecticut, for example, prohibits surveillance or monitoring "in areas designed for the health or personal comfort of the employees or for the safeguarding of their possessions, such as rest rooms, locker rooms or lounges." Moreover, state tort law may protect employees against highly offensive intrusions upon privacy in a place where a person has a reasonable expectation of privacy. For example, monitoring an employee bathroom may be considered an invasion of privacy.

Government employees have more rights in the area of employee

monitoring, since they have constitutional protections against unreasonable searches. These protections are discussed in Chapter 7.

• **Off-duty conduct.** Employers generally have wide latitude to
regulate employees' off-duty conduct. A few states, such as New
York and Colorado, prohibit employers from discriminating against
employees for their lawful off-duty conduct. About 20 states prohibit employment discrimination for employees' off-duty use of tobacco. Several other states prohibit discrimination because of the
off-duty use of any lawful substance.

Over 20 states prohibit employment discrimination based on
marital status, and about 10 states prohibit discrimination based
on sexual orientation.

WHAT ABOUT SEARCHES?

Unless there's a collective bargaining agreement restricting an employer's
right to search employees, searches are generally allowable. An employer
should be extremely careful, however, about how it conducts such searches—
it could be liable for a long list of torts, including assault, battery, false arrest,
intentional infliction of emotional harm, and invasion of privacy.

First, employers should have a work-related reason for the search. (This
does not mean they have to prove **probable cause,** a standard for lawful
searches in criminal cases that hinges on whether, under the facts, a reasonable person would believe that items implicating a crime are apt to be
found.) Second, any search should be conducted by the least intrusive
means possible. Third, employers should inform employees that searches
might be conducted. Fourth, employers should not physically harm employees in the course of the search or threaten employees with physical harm.
Last, employers should not attempt to prevent employees from leaving the
premises by threat of harm or other coercive means, although they are usually allowed to tell employees that they may be disciplined or discharged if
they leave.

---

forbid employers from disciplining employees because they have tried to enforce rights provided to them under the law. These provisions are discussed in Chapter 4, in the section dealing with anti-retaliation laws.

Otherwise, employers are generally free to determine disciplinary offenses. Employers often give employees a list of punishable offenses, either through posting on an employee bulletin board or in an employee handbook. They don't have to provide a list, however. They are free to make case-by-case determinations about workplace offenses.

Also, employers are generally free to decide the punishment for each workplace offense. One employer may decide that sleeping on the job merits a week's suspension whereas another employer will issue a written warning. Nor do employers have to issue a warning before imposing discipline. Employers can fire employees for committing a workplace offense, even for the first violation and even if the employees have good performance records.

Sometimes, however, employers impose limitations on themselves. Some states, for example, will enforce the limitations on discipline found in employer manuals. To be enforceable, the manuals must be given to the employees and the language relating to discipline must be clear and unambiguous.

For example, manual language stating "the following list of offenses may subject the employee to discipline" would not be sufficiently clear to limit the offenses for which discipline is imposed. However, a statement that "employees will be disciplined only for the following offenses" could be considered specific enough to be enforced. A statement that the employer will treat employees fairly during the disciplinary process is too vague to be enforced. But a statement that "no employee will be discharged unless he first receives a written warning" could prevent an employer from firing an employee without first giving a warning.

Whatever offenses an employer decides are punishable, and whatever the punishments it imposes, **Title VII** and other antidiscrimination laws require that rules and punishments be uniformly applied. The basic rule is that similarly situated people must be treated the same.

If a white employee is given a warning for cursing a supervisor, an Hispanic employee with a similar employment record committing the same offense could not be fired. Such a difference in treatment would be viewed as being based on the employee's race, and thus a violation of Title VII.

Similarly, Title VII would be violated by disciplining a woman who missed work, but not disciplining a man who was absent. Differences in treatment are allowed, however, if the employees are not similarly situated. Suppose the man who was absent brought a doctor's note justifying his absenteeism, while the woman did not have a legitimate excuse. In that case, an employer could discipline the woman and not the man without running afoul of Title VII. The difference in treatment is due to the difference in their circumstance—they are not similarly situated.

Federal and state laws might limit the methods an employer uses to investigate whether employees have violated workplace rules. (And, as discussed earlier in this chapter, monitoring or searching employees may subject the employer to state tort liability for invasion of privacy or intentional infliction of emotional distress.)

The **Employee Polygraph Protection Act (EPPA)** regulates using lie detectors to investigate employees' misconduct. This federal law establishes protections that apply nationwide. Some states may have laws giving workers even more protection.

Under the EPPA, lie detectors may be used only "in connection with an ongoing investigation which involves economic loss or injury to the employer's business." Thus, an employer could use a polygraph to determine if an employee had embezzled money, but not to find out if he had cursed his supervisor. Employers involved in making or distributing controlled substances (i.e., drugs) are allowed to use polygraphs to investigate "loss or injury to the manufacture, distribution or dispensing of any such controlled substance."

A second protection is that employees asked to take polygraph tests must have had access to the missing or damaged property. Also, an employer must have a reasonable suspicion that an employee is involved in the incident. Mere access to the property in question is not enough to support reasonable suspicion. (However, an employer who manufactures, distributes or dispenses controlled substances does not have to prove reasonable suspicion of the employee's involvement; mere access to the property is sufficient.)

Even if the employer complies with these two requirements, procedural limitations are still placed on using a polygraph. Before the test is given, the employee must be given reasonable written notice of its time and his right to consult an attorney before the test. The employee must also be told that he cannot be required to take the test as a condition of employment and that he can terminate the test at any time. The employer must explain the nature of the test and provide the employee with an opportunity to review the questions to be asked during the test.

During the test, the employee cannot be asked any questions about: religious or political beliefs, opinions regarding racial matters, opinions or activities involving labor unions, or any matter relating to sexual behavior.

The EPPA prohibits an employer from using the results of a polygraph test as the sole basis for imposing discipline; the employer is required to have additional supporting evidence. Before taking any disciplinary action, the employer must interview the employee based on the test results, and provide the employee with a written copy of the analysis of the test results.

HEALTH INSURANCE

No law requires an employer to provide health insurance. But if an employer does provide this benefit, it must be made available to all employees and administered without discrimination.

If an employer provides health insurance, **Title VII** requires that the insurance cover pregnancy and pregnancy-related conditions. Moreover, pregnancy and pregnancy-related conditions must be eligible for the same level of benefits as any other covered medical condition. Title VII does not, however, require that benefits cover abortions, "except where the life of the mother would be endangered if the fetus were carried to term, or except where medical complications have arisen from an abortion."

What if an employer's health insurance plan covers not only employees but their spouses and dependents? Then benefits do not have to be the same as the benefits provided *to the employees themselves,* but they must be the same for all spouses or for all dependents. Title VII requires that if the medical conditions of female employees' spouses are covered, then all male employees' spouses must have their medical conditions covered, including pregnancy and pregnancy-related conditions. However, the pregnancy of dependents need not be covered.

Under the **Age Discrimination in Employment Act (ADEA),** the employer must provide the same health insurance benefits to older workers as it does for younger employees. Benefits cannot be lowered because an employee becomes eligible for Medicare.

THIS COBRA DOESN'T BITE

A federal law with an unlikely acronym gives you important rights when you've lost a job or lost insurance because your work hours have been reduced. The **Consolidated Omnibus Budget Reconciliation Act of 1985 (COBRA)** applies to employers with 20 or more employees that offer group health insurance plans. (Churches and the federal government aren't covered.) An employee who loses health insurance because his or her employment is terminated, or his or her work hours reduced, can choose to continue coverage for a period of up to 18 months. However, the employee can be required to pay the full premium cost (even if previously the employer had picked up all or part of the premium cost), and can be charged an administrative fee of no more than 2 percent of the premium cost.

USERRA requires that the same health insurance continuation rights found in COBRA be available to employees on uniformed service leave. USERRA, moreover, applies to all employers, even those with fewer than 20 employees.

The **ADA** also impacts on health insurance. Employers cannot deny employees with disabilities equal access to health insurance coverage. Thus, if employees are eligible for health insurance, the employer cannot deny the same health insurance to an employee who is blind.

The ADA does not, however, require that health insurance cover all medical expenses or all disabilities. Limitations that affect both employees with disabilities and those without are permitted. **Pre-existing conditions** clauses, which disallow coverage for medical conditions that an individual had before being employed by the current employer, are lawful under the ADA. Limitations on coverage for certain procedures or treatments are also allowed, so long as the limitation is for a broad category of illnesses and not a specific disability or group of disabilities. For example, a plan limiting reimbursement for psychiatric treatment to 12 sessions a year would be lawful, but limiting psychiatric treatment to 12 sessions only for schizophrenia

---

THE IMPACT OF CHANGING JOBS ON HEALTH INSURANCE COVERAGE

Many employer group health insurance policies have clauses (called **preexisting condition** clauses) that limit or exclude coverage for medical conditions which were diagnosed before an individual enrolled in the health plan. With the passage of the **Health Insurance Portability and Accountability Act of 1996** (effective July 1, 1997), the impact of such preexisting condition clauses has been limited. Individuals with a preexisting medical condition that was diagnosed, or for which treatment was received, within six months before enrolling in a new health insurance plan would not be covered for that condition for the first 12 months. Thereafter, however, the preexisting condition would be covered for as long as the employee kept the insurance. Moreover, the 12-month exclusion period is reduced by the

would not. Similarly, excluding coverage for all eye care would be lawful, but excluding coverage only for glaucoma would be unlawful. Lastly, caps on reimbursement are lawful, unless the plan distinguishes among specific diseases. A plan that caps reimbursement for cancer or AIDS treatment at $50,000 but has a $1 million lifetime limit for other treatment would probably violate the ADA.

A health insurance plan containing a disability-based distinction may be lawful if the employer can prove that the plan meets the requirements of a bona fide benefit plan that is not a subterfuge for violating the ADA. The EEOC's interim guidance memorandum states that a distinction may be justified by proof "that the disability-based disparate treatment is attributable to the application of legitimate risk classification and underwriting procedures to the increased risks (and thus increased cost to the health insurance plan) of the disability, and not to the disability per se."

---

length, if any, of the individual's prior coverage under another health insurance policy. Lastly, a preexisting condition clause can never be applied to pregnancy, newborns, or adopted children.

For example, an employee worked for Employer A for five years, during which time he was covered under the employer's group health insurance plan. The employee quits his job and starts work for Employer B, which provides group health insurance for its employees. Employer B's health insurance plan could not apply any preexisting condition clause to that employee because his prior coverage under Employer A's plan exceeded the 12-month maximum exclusion allowed by law. If, however, an individual who had not previously been covered under a health insurance policy began working for Employer B, B's health insurance plan could apply its preexisting condition exclusion to that employee for a 12-month period.

SAFETY ON THE JOB

The **OSH Act** is a federal law whose purpose is to "assure so far as possible every working man and woman . . . safe and healthful working conditions." It applies to almost all private sector employers, but not to government employers.

The OSH Act imposes three obligations on employers.

First, employers are required to furnish a workplace "free from recognized hazards that are causing or are likely to cause death or serious physical harm" to employees.

Second, employers are required to comply with the safety and health standards promulgated by the **Occupational Safety and Health Administration (OSHA),** the federal agency charged with enforcing the law.

An example of an OSHA regulation is the **Hazard Communication Standard.** This standard requires that employees who work with hazardous chemicals be informed of the types of chemicals with which they are working and be trained in their handling. Chemical manufacturers and distributors are required to label containers identifying any hazardous chemicals and give appropriate hazard warnings. Employers who use such hazardous chemicals in the workplace are required to develop a written hazard communication program for their employees. As part of this program the employer must compile a list of all hazardous chemicals used in the workplace; identify the physical and health hazards associated with these chemicals; state precautions to be used in handling the chemicals; and indicate emergency and first aid procedures to be used in the event of a problem. This information must be made available to employees. Employees must also receive training in detecting the presence of chemicals in the workplace and protecting themselves from these hazards.

Other OSHA regulations limit employees' exposure to toxic substances, require that employees wear personal protective equipment (like hard hats or respirators) when performing certain types of work, and require fire protection systems in the workplace.

The third OSH Act requirement is that employers with 11 or more employees are required to maintain a log and summary of all occupational injuries and illnesses, along with supplemental records detailing each illness and injury.

Employees who believe there is a health or safety hazard at work can either notify their supervisor or the company safety director or contact OSHA and request an inspection. (Issues relating to OSHA inspections are discussed in Appendix II.)

Sometimes, however, the hazard poses such an imminent threat to employees' health or safety that there is no time to contact OSHA. The OSH Act protects a worker who refuses to perform a job that is likely to cause imminent death or serious injury. Generally, employees do not have a right to refuse to perform work, and normally an employer could discipline or discharge an employee for such a refusal. However, under the OSH Act, an employer is prohibited from discharging or disciplining an employee who refuses to perform work that the employee believes in good faith poses a real danger of death or serious injury, *if* all of the following factors are present:

1. a reasonable person in the employee's position would also conclude that there is a real danger of death or serious injury;
2. there is insufficient time to eliminate the danger through regular OSHA channels; and
3. the employee has unsuccessfully asked the employer to fix the problem.

States may also regulate workplace health and safety in two ways. First, they may have regulations covering workplace conditions that are not dealt with by OSHA standards. Second, they may adopt a state safety and health plan that at minimum duplicates the requirements of the OSH Act (it may also provide for higher standards), and if approved by OSHA, the state would then be responsible for enforcing safety and health regulations within its borders. OSHA has approved about 25 state health and safety plans. In the absence of approval by OSHA, however, a state may not regulate any safety and health issue that is already regulated by the OSH Act.

COMPENSATION FOR JOB-RELATED INJURY AND ILLNESS

Workers' compensation laws provide money to pay for medical expenses and replace income lost as a result of employment injuries and illnesses. The employee is not required to prove that the injuries were caused by some negligence of the employer in order to recover under the workers' compensation laws. These laws impose **strict liability** on employers for injuries suffered at the workplace. In this context, strict liability means that employers are liable even if they are not at fault. The rationale is that this places the burden of paying for injuries on the party most able to bear the cost. The trade-off for employers is that benefits under workers' compensation are limited (no "pain and suffering" or punitive damages, for example) so employers are spared expensive surprises. The trade-off for employees is that they are assured of receiving some monetary remedy for workplace injuries, though they are limited to the workers' compensation system as the exclusive means for receiving compensation. Generally speaking, employees cannot sue employers under state tort law to recover damages for workplace injuries.

PERMANENT DISABILITY AND DEATH

If you suffer a permanent disability, whether partial or total, you are also eligible for a payment to compensate for the decrease in earnings attributable to the permanent nature of the disability. The amount you'll get may be determined by a **schedule** (a list that specifies wage loss for specific disabilities, for example, $8,910 for loss of an index finger), or by percentage of weekly wage.

If a workplace injury results in your death, money is generally provided to your spouse and children. Death benefits consist of a burial allowance and a percentage of your weekly wages. There may be a maximum cap on benefits. Death benefits are provided to a spouse until remarriage, and to the children until they reach majority.

Each state has its own law regarding workers' compensation benefits. The general requirements of the laws are similar, although the dollar amounts recoverable and certain procedural and coverage details vary by state. There are separate federal workers' compensation laws covering federal government employees, employees of the railroad and maritime industries, and longshoremen and harbor workers.

The cost of providing workers' compensation is borne solely by the employer, usually through buying a workers' compensation insurance policy from an insurance company. The cost of providing this insurance cannot be deducted from an employee's wages.

Most employees injured at work are entitled to compensation under these laws. Some state laws exempt certain categories of workers, such as casual employees, agricultural employees, domestic employees, and independent contractors. Moreover, a few states require coverage only if an employer employs a minimum number of employees; for example, Alabama imposes compulsory coverage only if an employer has at least three employees.

Injuries and illnesses that "arise out of and in the course of employment" are covered. This means that there must be some connection between an employment requirement and the cause of the injury. An automobile accident occurring during the commute to work is not covered, but a traveling salesperson who is in an accident while on her way to a sales call would be compensated.

Examples of **compensable injuries** include injuries caused by defective machinery, fires or explosions at work, repeated lifting of heavy equipment, or slipping on an oily floor surface at work. **Compensable illnesses** or **occupational diseases** are illnesses caused by working conditions, where the job presents a greater risk of contracting the illness than the normal risks of everyday life. A clerical worker who contracts emphysema from secondhand smoke and works in an office with coworkers who smoke would probably not be compensated for the illness, because there is nothing peculiar about her job that increased the risk of contracting emphysema. A textile worker, however, who contracts brown lung disease would be eligible for compensation.

The amount of money paid for an injury or illness varies by state and is based on the type of injury or illness. Workers receive a fixed weekly benefit based on their regular salary, generally in the 50 to 66 percent range. This wage payment is made for the period during which the employee is temporarily unable to work due to the injury.

Workers' compensation also pays for all medical expenses associated with the injury or illness. Most state laws also provide some reimbursement for the costs associated with medical and vocational rehabilitation.

To collect workers' compensation benefits, employees usually must notify the employer as soon as possible after they have sustained an injury. In most states, they then file a claim with the employer or the employer's insurance agent. If the employer does not contest a claim, it proposes a settlement to the employee. If the employee accepts the settlement, payment begins.

What if the employer contests the claim or the employee rejects the settlement? Then the claim is usually filed with the state workers' compensation commission, which holds a hearing to determine whether the employee is entitled to benefits and, if so, the amount due. The commission's decision can be appealed to state court.

The **federal social security disability insurance system** also provides compensation for injuries that prevent an employee from working. This system differs from workers' compensation in that the cause of the injury is irrelevant for purposes of social security. Under workers' compensation, an injury must arise out of employment, but for purposes of receiving money under social security, the injury need only prevent a person from being able to work (regardless of the cause of the injury). Thus, while the automobile accident on the commute to work is not compensable under workers' compensation, a worker may be eligible for social security benefits if accident injuries prevent the worker from earning a living.

An employee in a job covered by social security is eligible to receive benefits for a disabling injury or illness if the employee has at least six quarters of coverage. A quarter of coverage is a calender quarter in which an employee earns a minimum wage amount as determined by the secretary of health and human services. Generally, social security covers every worker, except for certain federal employees, like postal workers and railroad employees.

A **disabling medical condition** is one that is expected to last at least 12 months and prevent someone from gainfully working anywhere in the country. **The Social Security Administration (SSA)** has published a list of impairments that are considered disabling, such as severe epilepsy and loss of vision or hearing. A medical condition that does not appear on the list may still be considered disabling if the worker can show that the condition is the medical equivalent of a listed impairment—that it is equal in severity and duration to a listed impairment. If an injury or illness cannot be shown to be the medical equivalent of a listed impairment, workers may still be eligible for benefits if they can prove by another means that they have a disabling medical condition. They would have to show that the condition or disease is so severe that it prevents them from performing their job or other similar work; this is extremely difficult to prove.

To collect social security disability insurance benefits, a disabled employee must file an application at the local social security office. The SSA decides whether an employee is eligible for benefits. If the SSA decides in favor of the employee, he or she will receive a letter detailing the benefits to be received and payment dates. If the SSA denies benefits, the employee can request a reconsideration of the decision. If the reconsideration is still unfavorable, he or she can file an appeal and request a hearing before an administrative law judge. The decision of the administrative law judge is appealable to an Appeals Council, whose decision can in turn be appealed to federal court.

■

CHAPTER FOUR

Ending the Employment Relationship

Leaving Your Job—Voluntarily or Not

N O JOB LASTS FOREVER. You usually leave a job for one of four reasons: you're fired or laid off, or you retire or quit. The law affects each of these endings.

BEING FIRED

In the United States, most of us are considered **employees at will.** This means that we have no written contract governing the length of our employment or the reasons for which we might lose our jobs. The employer is free to fire us with no notice and with no reason. And we are free to leave the job at will.

Three major categories of employees, however, are not employed at will. The first group consists of a small number of workers, usually executives and highly skilled professionals, who have a written contract setting forth a length of employment and prohibiting discharge except under specified circumstances. These contracts are enforceable in state court.

The second group consists of employees represented by unions and covered by collective bargaining agreements. These agreements normally provide that employees can be discharged only for **just cause** (a phrase whose precise meaning might vary from contract to contract, but certainly limits the employer's unfettered right to fire). Moreover, collective bargaining agreements contain grievance mechanisms. These give union employees a way to challenge their firing. Collective bargaining agreements are discussed in detail in Chapter 6.

The third group consists of government employees, who are protected by civil service laws. These laws normally require the employer to have just cause in order to terminate employment. Government employees can appeal discharge decisions through civil service commissions. Civil service laws are discussed in more detail in Chapter 7.

There are two other exceptions to the general rule that employees can be terminated at will. One state has passed a law giving workers protection from being arbitrarily fired. Montana has enacted the **Wrongful Discharge from Employment Act,** which expressly prohibits firing nonprobationary employees except for good cause. **Good cause** is defined as "reasonable job-related grounds for dismissal" for legitimate business reasons.

The other exception applies to those situations where federal or state law has placed a specific restriction on the employer's power to fire. These restrictions, which are described below, apply to only a limited category of cases.

ANTIDISCRIMINATION LAWS

Title VII, the **ADEA,** the **ADA, USERRA,** and the **NLRA** all prohibit employers from firing workers if the reason for the decision is membership in a protected class or union activity. **ERISA** also protects employees from being fired if the object is to prevent them from accruing pension and welfare benefits.

Many state laws contain a broader range of protected classes or activities. States like Wisconsin, California, and Michigan prohibit firings based, for example, on weight, height, sexual orientation, marital status, and arrest record. As discussed in Chapter 3, many state laws prohibit firings for off-duty conduct, such as smoking, drinking, or political activity.

USERRA provides a special protection against firing. The broad prohibition against being fired because you are or have been a member of the uniformed services is supplemented by a special provision dealing with employees reinstated to their jobs after a leave of absence for military duty. USERRA provides that a person who is reemployed cannot be fired *except for cause* within one year after reemployment, as long as the employee's period of military service was more than 180 days. You can't be fired *except for cause* within 180 days after reemployment if your period of military service was more than 30 days but less than 181 days.

ANTI-RETALIATION LAWS

Effectively enforcing labor and employment laws requires help from the employees themselves. Employees are in the best position to know what happens in the workplace and whether or not their rights have been violated. Many enforcement agencies depend mainly on complaints from employees to alert them to violations of the law.

Employees are particularly vulnerable, however, when it comes to making complaints. Their economic livelihood depends on the employer, which has the authority to discipline and discharge them. Understandably, employees may be reluctant to stand up for their rights, or make complaints, for fear that they will lose their jobs.

FIRING MEMBERS OF A PROTECTED CLASS

In determining if a discharge violates the antidiscrimination laws, the issue is whether the employer's reason was the worker's membership in a protected class or whether it was for some other (any other) reason. Merely belonging to a protected class does not grant immunity from being fired. But being in a protected class means that you must be treated the same as workers not in the protected class when employers decide what types of conduct warrant discharge and when to impose discharge as a penalty. As with employee discipline, the basic rule is that similarly situated people must be treated the same. (See discussion on employee discipline in Chapter 3.)

Because of potential retaliation against employees who enforce their statutory rights, all federal labor and employment laws (with the exception of **WARN**; see page 86), and most state labor and employment laws, specifically prohibit employers from disciplining or discharging employees because they have attempted to enforce their rights under the law. Enforcing their rights includes filing a complaint with the agency that enforces the law, helping the agency investigate a complaint, and participating in a proceeding to enforce rights under the law (such as testifying or filing a lawsuit).

The anti-retaliation clause contained in **Title VII,** the **ADEA** and the **ADA** offers a broader scope of protection than most standard anti-retaliation provisions. Title VII, the ADEA and the ADA protect not only employee **participation activity** (activity that constitutes enforcing rights), but also **opposition activity.** Employers cannot discriminate against an employee because "he has opposed any practice made unlawful" under either Title VII, the ADEA or the ADA. Employees who complain to their employer about discrimination in the workplace, or who take part in demonstrations protesting employment discrimination, are protected from retaliation under Title VII, the ADEA and the ADA.

WHISTLE-BLOWER PROTECTION

Over 30 states have passed **whistle-blower laws.** These laws prohibit employers from firing employees who report suspected violations of state or federal laws, rules or regulations. The whistle-blower laws are much broader in scope than the anti-retaliation laws.

The anti-retaliation provisions are limited to the enforcement of the specific rights contained in that statute. For example, the anti-retaliation provision in Title VII protects employees who file a complaint alleging that their rights *under Title VII* have been violated. The whistle-blower laws, on the other hand, do not limit their protection to reporting violations of a particular law. Under many state whistle-blower laws, as long as employees are reporting a suspected violation of *any* law, they are protected.

Second, the anti-retaliation laws are linked specifically to laws dealing with the workplace. For example, OSHA's anti-retaliation clause protects employees who complain about safety and health issues at work. The whistle-blower laws, on the other hand, are not limited to the workplace. A construction worker who reported that his employer was paying off a housing inspector would be protected under these laws.

The scope of the whistle-blower laws varies considerably by state. Most states protect only government employees, but a significant number also protect private sector workers. Also, sometimes these laws protect employees only when they report the violation to particular persons. Some laws protect employees who disclose information either to the employer or to an appropriate government agency. Other laws protect employees only when the report is made to a government agency.

There is also a whistle-blower law that protects federal government workers. The **Whistleblower Protection Act** prohibits federal government agency employers from retaliating against employees for disclosing any information that the employee reasonably believes provides evidence of a violation of any law, rule or regulation.

STATE COMMON-LAW EXCEPTIONS TO EMPLOYMENT AT WILL

As mentioned at the beginning of this chapter, the employment at will doctrine governs most cases of employee termination. Most state courts, however, have identified certain situations where the employer's otherwise complete right of discharge is limited. These are the public policy exception and the enforcement of implied contracts.

Over 30 state courts have adopted the **public policy exception** to the employment at will doctrine. This exception makes the employer liable to personal injury suits for damages caused to an employee whose termination is contrary to the underlying public policy of the state. **Public policy** "is that principle of law that holds that no subject can lawfully do that which has a tendency to be injurious to the public, or against the public good. . . ." The public policy of a state can generally be found in the state constitution, laws and regulations and sometimes state court decisions.

Courts recognize four kinds of firing that have public policy implications.

First, firing an employee who refuses to perform an illegal act is contrary to public policy. The employer that fired an employee for refusing to commit perjury (see box below) fell within this class of cases.

A second kind of offense against public policy is firing an employee who reports a violation of the law. This is similar to the protection extended under state whistle-blower laws. An example is an eyeglass manufacturer that fires an employee who reports to the federal Food and Drug Administration that the company is not performing legally required tests for determining lenses' resistance to shattering.

A third type of case involves firing an employee for engaging in acts that public policy encourages. For example, an employee who voluntarily cooperates with government authorities investigating possible antitrust violations would be protected from discharge. In this situation there is no law requiring the employee to cooperate, so failure to do so would not be an illegal act. Also, the employee is not actually reporting a violation of the antitrust laws, so the

---

THE IMPORTANCE OF PUBLIC POLICY

The courts justify the public policy exception by reasoning that employers should not be allowed to use their economic power over employees in a way that undermines the interests of the community as a whole, or that is injurious to the public good. For example, one of the first cases dealing with this exception involved an employer that instructed one of its employees to testify falsely before a state legislative committee. When the employee refused to commit perjury, he was discharged. The court held that the employer's use of its authority to undermine the policy of the state could be punished by personal injury lawsuits.

---

second type of exception would not apply. However, helping the government enforce its laws inures to the good of the public as a whole. Thus, an employer's attempt to stop an employee from cooperating would be viewed as against the public good.

The fourth class of cases deals with firing an employee for exercising statutory rights. This is very similar to the protection offered under the anti-retaliation provisions of the labor laws. For example, an employer firing employees who have filed workers' compensation claims is attempting to undermine the state's policy that injured workers should receive compensation.

States recognizing the public policy exception do not necessarily recognize it in all four types of cases. A few states do recognize all four, and most recognize the exception for refusing to perform an illegal act and exercising a statutory right. About six states, including Alabama, Georgia, and Florida, have rejected any attempt to modify the strict common-law employment at will doctrine, and do not recognize any public policy exception.

The second exception to the employment at will doctrine deals with **implied contracts.** Most state courts have recognized that an employer's promises that limit when it will terminate its employees can be binding and enforceable. Such promises can be the result of statements found in manuals and handbooks, or oral statements made directly by the employer to the employee.

Many employers have created personnel manuals or handbooks that contain the policies and procedures governing the employment relationship. These may include the procedures and reasons for discharge. As noted earlier (see Chapter 3), the statements contained in these handbooks can be enforced if manuals are given to employees and contain clear and specific language regarding the circumstances for discharge. A vague statement like "All employees will be treated fairly; in most cases employees will be warned before they are discharged" is not enforceable. More specific language that may be enforceable is: "No employee will be discharged without good cause; employees will only be fired if they violate one of the following rules" (with the rules specified).

Employers can avoid creating binding promises by clearly and unambiguously informing employees that the policies contained in the handbook are not meant to create a contract.

Even when the requirements for a binding contract are present, employers remain free to revoke or revise the policies contained in the handbook. Once they give notice to employees that a policy has been changed, the old policy is no longer enforceable for situations arising after the change.

A few courts will enforce oral promises of job security, but they are very difficult to prove. Usually, such promises must be made specifically to the employee, and not in a statement or announcement made to workers generally. Also, these promises must generally be made during preemployment interviews, when the employer uses them as incentives to get the employee to accept the job. In other words, the employee has reasonably relied on the promise and accepted the job in part because of it. Last, the wording of the promise must be very specific. Vague promises of "permanent" employment or "the job is yours so long as you perform" will typically not be enforced. It is extremely helpful in such cases to have additional objective evidence (such as memoranda or handbooks) to support the oral promise.

BEING LAID OFF

While the effects of a discharge and a layoff may be the same (an employee is out of work), the reasons are usually different. A **discharge** is

---

PROTECTING AGAINST IMPLIED CONTRACTS

Many employers attempt to escape the problem of creating oral contracts by including written statements on their application forms to the effect that if the employee is hired, he or she is employed at will, can be discharged at any time for any reason, and that no individual within the company is authorized to make any promises to the contrary.

---

usually the result of some conduct of the employee—the employee's performance was not up to standard; the employee violated company work rules; or the employee's personality conflicted with those of others in the workplace. A **layoff,** however, usually results from the operation of the business—sales are down and the employer does not need as many workers; a merger has resulted in duplication among workers; or the company has reorganized and certain types of jobs are no longer needed. There is usually less stigma attached to a layoff than to a discharge. Also, a laid-off employee may be recalled if business improves. A fired worker won't.

No specific law governs either how employees can be laid off or the way of selecting who will be laid off. If there is no collective bargaining agreement establishing layoff procedures (see Chapter 6), an employer is generally free to determine when layoffs are necessary and who is to be laid off. Contrary to popular belief, an employer is not required to use seniority (as in last hired, first laid off) to determine layoffs. Nor does the law require the employer to pay severance to laid-off workers.

FAIR WARNING

The **Worker Adjustment and Retraining Notification Act (WARN)** requires employers to give 60 days' advance notice of mass layoffs and plant closings. WARN is a federal law that applies to private sector employers with 100 or more employees. Employers must provide notice to workers, their unions, and state and local government officials. A **mass layoff** is defined as a reduction in force that results in the layoff of: at least 33 percent of the workforce and at least 50 employees; or at least 500 employees. Failure to give 60 days' notice may make an employer liable for back pay and any benefits due under an employee benefit plan, for each day that the notice was not given.

Of course, as with all areas of employment, the employer's freedom is restricted by antidiscrimination laws. The employer may not decide which employees to lay off based on their membership in a protected class.

Concerns about age discrimination often come up in layoffs. Mass layoffs disproportionately reducing the number of older workers may indicate that age discrimination is involved. Employers cannot base a layoff decision on the assumption that older workers are not as productive as younger workers, or on the belief that "young blood" is necessary for new ideas. However, decisions can be made based on the performance and evaluation of the specific workers involved.

Sometimes, to encourage employees to voluntarily quit rather than face layoff, employers offer incentive packages. These packages usually contain additional economic inducements not generally available to laid-off employees. They often require employees to waive their right to sue the company for anything that happened while they were employed. Such **waivers** are enforceable, as long as they are knowing and voluntary, and can prevent an employee from suing the company for any violations of labor and employment laws. There is one exception to the general enforceability of knowing and voluntary waivers—courts will not enforce a waiver of any claims that arise under the **FLSA**.

The courts usually consider several factors in deciding whether a waiver is **knowing and voluntary:**

1. Is the waiver written in a way that can be understood by the employee?
2. Did the employee receive a benefit in exchange for the waiver that he or she was not already entitled to receive? and
3. Did the employee have a reasonable time to consider the offer?

If a waiver includes waiving the right to file a lawsuit under the **ADEA,** a very specific list of requirements must be met. Besides the requirements for a voluntary waiver listed above, the ADEA also requires that: the waiver specifically refer to the ADEA; the waiver does not waive rights arising after the waiver is signed; the employee is advised in writing to consult an attorney; the individual is given at least 21 days to consider the waiver before signing; and the waiver can be revoked within seven days after it is signed.

RETIRING

The ADEA has outlawed mandatory retirement. That means that employees cannot be forced to retire at any age except for three categories of employees: police, firefighters and certain executives. Police and firefighters who are employed by either state or local governments can be forced to retire if there is a state or local law in effect as of March 3, 1983, that establishes a mandatory retirement age (or if there is no law, if the employee is 55 years old) and retirement is pursuant to a bona fide retirement plan. The exception for executives applies to individuals employed for at least two years before their forced retirement as bona fide executives or high policy-making employees. These executives can be forced to retire at the age of 65 (or later) if they are eligible to receive an immediate, nonforfeitable annual retirement benefit of at least $44,000.

Except for these three classes of workers, no employer covered by the ADEA can force an employee to retire. Small employers not covered by the ADEA are usually covered by state age discrimination laws prohibiting mandatory retirement.

Employers may, however, offer *voluntary* retirement packages to employees, as long as acceptance is truly voluntary. Employers usually make such offers as a way to downsize the workforce and avoid involuntary layoffs. The ADEA specifically allows an employer to offer such packages to classes of workers based on, among other things, their age, without violating the provisions of the ADEA prohibiting different treatment based on age. Thus, the fact that the voluntary retirement package is offered only to employees who are 55 years of age and older is not illegal discrimination against individuals who are 52 years old. When part of the voluntary retirement package includes a waiver of the right to sue under the ADEA, the waiver must be knowing and voluntary and meet the requirements discussed in the preceding section dealing with waivers during a layoff.

QUITTING

In the absence of a written contract limiting a worker's right to quit, the employee is free to quit at any time and for any reason. But if there is a written contract, the employee must comply with any requirements limiting the right to quit.

Employees are not required by law to give any type of notice prior to quitting. It is usually a good idea to do so, however, as a matter of common employment courtesy.

SOME OTHER ISSUES

Regardless of how employment ends, several related issues commonly arise: mitigation; payment of wages owed; references for future employment; covenants not to compete; and eligibility for unemployment compensation.

MITIGATION

Mitigation in the context of labor law most often means that employees who think they've been unjustly terminated must take active steps to seek new employment. In its general legal meaning, **mitigation** refers to steps taken to lessen the damage that has occurred as the result of wrongful conduct. For example, a landlord whose tenant has skipped six months early on the lease had better make an effort to rent the now-vacant property. If the landlord does not take steps to limit the loss caused by the tenant's departure, a judge might find the tenant not liable for the full amount of the rent due.

A general principle in labor law requires an employee to mitigate the damages suffered as a result of an unlawful termination. An employee cannot just sit back and wait until an administrative agency or court rules in her favor. Failing to look for a new job can affect the amount of damages awarded to the employee in court. Employees claiming they have been unlawfully terminated must use reasonable diligence to find equivalent employment with another employer. Employees are not required to go into another line of work, accept a demotion or take a demeaning position, but if they do not look for, or if they refuse, a job substantially equivalent to the one they had, they may forfeit their right to back pay.

GETTING WHAT YOU'RE OWED

While no federal law regulates this subject, almost every state has passed a law that sets a deadline for paying accrued wages when employees leave. These laws are usually referred to as **wage payment statutes.** About half the states require that unpaid wages must be paid no later than the next regular pay period. Other states set a specific time period that runs from the date of separation—for example, within three days of termination. The time period specified in these laws ranges from immediately to 15 days.

What are **wages** under these laws? Most of them define wages as not only earned but unpaid salary, but also earned but unused vacation pay, and severance pay when the employer's policy provides for severance pay as a benefit of employment. Neither federal nor state law requires employers to provide severance pay as a benefit of employment, but if employers do so the wage payment laws specify when severance must be paid.

REFERENCES

Generally, employers are not legally required to provide a reference. A few states are exceptions. For example, Indiana, Missouri and Kansas have **service letter** acts. These acts require that, upon the request of the terminated employee, the employer must provide a letter that states the nature of the employee's job, the length of employment and the reason for separation.

Employers providing references must be aware of certain legal implications. Most states have blacklisting statutes. **Blacklisting** consists of intentionally trying to prevent someone from obtaining employment. However, truthful statements about someone's ability to perform the job in question are not considered to be blacklisting.

The Supreme Court has interpreted the anti-retaliation clause in **Title VII** to encompass giving a bad reference to a former employee because that person has filed a charge under Title VII.

The way a reference is made and its content can give rise to employer liability under state **tort** law. The employee may be able to recover damages for defamation, intentional interference with a prospective employment contract, intentional infliction of emotional distress, or negligent misrepresentation.

Defamation occurs when one person's false statement injures the reputation of another person. Providing false information to a prospective employer with the intent of causing an applicant to lose the job constitutes **intentional interference** with a prospective employment contract. False statements that cause a loss of money (i.e., a wage-paying job) can be grounds for **negligent misrepresentation.** The premise behind all of these tort actions is that the employer's statement is false. Making truthful statements concerning a former employee usually does not subject the employer to liability for defamation, interference with a contract or misrepresentation.

Moreover, most states recognize a **qualified privilege defense** to charges of defamation, even if the information provided by the employer turns out to be false. This means that if the employer was providing a reference in good faith to someone with a legitimate reason to ask for it, the employer will not be liable even for a false statement. However, the employer will lose the qualified privilege if

- it was motivated primarily by ill will in making the statement;
- it provided the information to individuals who did not have a legitimate reason to receive it; or
- the statement was made without grounds for believing it was true.

Disclosing even true information, moreover, can result in tort liability for **intentional infliction of emotional distress**. If the information is private and personal, the employee has a reasonable expectation that it will be kept private, and the information is unrelated to work, disclosing it may make the employer liable.

COVENANTS NOT TO COMPETE

Covenants not to compete are written contracts restricting workers' ability to compete against their former employer for a certain period of time and in a certain geographic area. For example, this kind of contract might provide that a financial advisor will not provide financial services to customers within a 25-mile radius of the employer's place of business for 12 months after leaving the company. These agreements prevent workers from being able to unfairly compete against their former employer because of:

- specialized knowledge unique to that employer and obtained while working for that employer (for example, trade secrets);
- access to customer lists that are not otherwise easily accessible; or
- specialized skills acquired while working for the employer.

GIVING REFERENCES SAFELY

Because of the potential pitfalls involved, many employers refuse to provide references. Others provide only basic information, such as verifying the former employee's dates of employment and job duties performed. Employers that do provide references can limit their exposure to liability by limiting the number of individuals authorized to provide references, avoiding statements based on hearsay or gossip, and discussing only issues that have a direct bearing on an individual's work.

Covenants not to compete are enforceable only if the employer has a substantial right unique to its business that it is trying to protect. Thus, a covenant between a retail store and an in-store salesperson based on that employee's access to customers would not be enforced because this would not be a unique or substantial interest of the employer. However, a covenant between a securities firm and one of its salespersons may be enforced.

Even a covenant seeking to protect a unique and substantial business right must be reasonable in terms of geographic area and time limits. Reasonableness depends on the specific facts of each case. Some general guidelines are that time limits of one year are reasonable, but over three years are not. Geographic limitations should be restricted to the area in which the employee had worked.

While most covenants not to compete are entered into when the employee is hired, sometimes an employer may require one as a condition of remaining employed. A few states will enforce only covenants that were executed when the employee was hired. Most states will enforce a covenant executed as a condition of continued employment as long as the employee actually worked for a reasonable period of time after signing the covenant. Some states require independent consideration (such as changes in salary and status) in addition to continued employment.

In considering covenants not to compete, courts attempt to balance the restrictions necessary to protect the employer's unique and substantial business interests against restrictions that are unduly harsh and limiting of an individual's ability to earn a livelihood. Courts can enforce valid covenants either by issuing an **injunction** preventing the former employee from working in violation of the covenant, or by awarding money to the former employer for losses resulting from the unfair competition.

UNEMPLOYMENT COMPENSATION

States administer the unemployment insurance system to provide workers and their families with weekly income during periods of unemployment. When workers are unemployed due to plant closure, layoff, natural disaster, or other acts or circumstances that are not their fault, they may be entitled to receive **unemployment compensation (UC).**

The system is funded by state and federal taxes paid by employers. Within federal guidelines, each state determines the scope and coverage of and eligibility for UC. Most workers are covered by the insurance system, but there are some exceptions. Generally excluded are: self-employed individuals, independent contractors, casual employees and agricultural workers.

To receive UC, a worker must meet certain eligibility requirements. These requirements vary among the states, but most states determine eligibility by four criteria:

1. the applicant must have earned a minimum amount of wages within a specified period and/or worked for a minimum period in the recent past (for example, at least 20 weeks of work at an average weekly wage of at least $20);
2. the applicant must register for work with the state unemployment office;
3. the applicant must be available for work; and
4. the applicant must be actively seeking employment.

Once employees meet the eligibility requirements, they may still be denied UC benefits because of a **disqualifying event.** As a general rule, workers are disqualified if they voluntarily quit without good cause or if they were fired for misconduct. In some states, the disqualification lasts for only a specified length of time, after which an employee can receive UC.

The meaning of **good cause** varies greatly among the states. Some states consider certain types of personal reasons as good cause for quitting—for example, having to care for a sick relative, or following a spouse who has found work in another state. Most states, however, require that good cause be due to the employer's actions. For example, working conditions that are so bad they would cause a reasonable person to quit would be considered good cause in some states. The **reasonable person** perspective is very important in determining good cause. It is not enough that a situation is intolerable to a specific worker. The conditions must be such that a reasonable person, in the same position as the employee, would feel compelled to quit.

The meaning of **misconduct** also varies by state, but generally incompetence alone is not considered misconduct. Violating known company rules and insubordination are examples of misconduct.

Since one of the eligibility requirements for UC is that the applicant is actively seeking work, an applicant who refuses a suitable job offer may become ineligible for benefits. It depends on why the worker refused. If the job was not suitable work, the refusal is acceptable. A job is not suitable if the worker has no experience for it, it is more hazardous than the worker's previous job, or the physical condition of the worker prevents him or her from accepting it.

States also consider travel costs and time, bad working hours, community wage levels, and compelling personal problems in deciding if a job may be rejected. Finally, workers usually cannot lose benefits for refusing a job offer that is made because the current workforce is on strike.

If wages and conditions of a new job are below those of a worker's old job, he or she may not have to accept it to remain eligible. For example, a skilled craftsperson is permitted to refuse a job as a janitor. After a certain period of time, however, most states require the worker to "lower his sights" and accept a lesser job.

Workers who are on strike and therefore out of work may be entitled to UC—it depends on the specific state law. A few states allow workers to collect UC if the strike is caused by an employer's violation of the **NLRA** or an employer's breach of the collective bargaining agreement. Some states allow workers to receive benefits if the employer has "locked out" the workers.

Most states, however, do not permit striking workers to collect benefits. The period of disqualification varies by state. In some states the disqualification lasts for the entire strike; in other states the disqualification lasts for a fixed period of time. If a striker is permanently replaced, however, the worker may then be eligible for benefits.

The amount of UC money that an individual receives varies by state. The general formula is 50 percent of the employee's weekly wage, not to exceed a statutory cap on the amount paid. The cap is based on a percentage of the state's average weekly wages for all workers. Because of the cap on maximum benefits, most workers receive much less than 50 percent of their weekly wage.

Usually UC benefits last 26 weeks. In times of extended high unemployment, however, benefits may be paid for an additional 13 weeks and sometimes longer.

If unemployed workers receive other benefits or income, the amounts are usually deducted from their UC payments. Some states ignore small amounts of money received, but most states will reduce or stop UC benefits for weeks in which an unemployed worker receives disability benefits, severance pay, or other types of income.

Workers moving to another state to look for work can still collect UC, because all states belong to the **Interstate Reciprocal Benefit Payment Plan.** This plan allows workers to register for work and file for UC in a new state. The law of the original state, however, determines eligibility for benefits. The worker must satisfy that state's requirements to receive UC in the new state.

HOW TO FILE FOR UNEMPLOYMENT COMPENSATION

To receive UC, you must file a claim for benefits at your local state unemployment office. File as soon as possible after unemployment begins, since you won't get benefits until all the paperwork is processed and eligibility for benefits is verified.

You should take the following documents with you to the unemployment office to help verify your eligibility: social security card, recent pay stubs, and any documents showing the reason for the job loss.

After filing the initial claim, you usually must report regularly to the unemployment office to verify your continued eligibility for benefits. You can lose benefits if you don't report.

■

CHAPTER FIVE

Retirement

Your Pension and Social Security Rights

THE MAJOR ISSUE facing us as we retire is having an adequate continuing source of income. Two major work-related systems provide postretirement income: pensions and social security. About half of all people who work for private companies are covered by a pension plan. More than 95 percent of American workers are eligible for social security.

PENSIONS

Employers are not required to provide pension benefits, but if they do, they can't discriminate against members of a protected class. In particular, even though actuarial tables show that women live longer than men, employers cannot provide different pension plans for each sex. In a **defined-contribution plan,** an employer must contribute the same amount for both males and females; in a **defined-benefit plan,** both males and females must receive the same benefit payout.

Employers are not, however, required to provide a pension to all their workers. They can exclude up to 30 percent of the workforce, and they can exclude certain types of employees, such as hourly workers and the secretarial staff. However, pensions cannot just cover the higher-ups in the organization, nor can they discriminate against lower-paid workers.

ERISA

The **Employee Retirement Income Security Act of 1974 (ERISA)**, a federal statute, is by far the most important pension law. ERISA covers most pension plans operated by private sector employers, but does not cover any government workers or the military. It applies to private sector employers whose plans are "qualified" under the federal tax laws or whose business affects interstate commerce. The tax laws provide important advantages to companies whose plans "qualify," so most pension plans are regulated by ERISA.

ERISA protects you if you participate in a pension plan. It also covers your beneficiaries. This federal law **preempts** any state laws that seek to regulate pension plans. That means that states have no power to regulate pension plans, though they can regulate how benefits are divided in divorce.

ERISA sets legal minimums that a pension plan must provide. An employer may, however, provide more liberal terms in its pension plan.

ERISA deals with the following aspects of pension plans: (1) participation; (2) benefit accrual, vesting and breaks in service; (3) funding; (4) administration of funds; (5) reporting and disclosure; (6) joint and survivor provisions; and (7) plan termination.

Participation ERISA requires that most workers be allowed to participate in an employer-sponsored pension plan if they are at least 21 years of age and have completed one year of service with the company. ERISA defines one year of service as a 12-month period during which you have worked 1,000 hours (considered half-time) or more.

Benefit Accrual You begin to accrue benefits under the plan once you qualify for participation. How benefits accrue depends on the type of pension plan.

A **defined-contribution plan** establishes a separate retirement account for each participating employee. A common kind of defined contribution plan is the **401(k) plan,** though there are others. In these plans, the employer (and sometimes the employee) makes a contribution to the account at least annually. Benefits are based on how investments have fared, so these accounts are riskier than defined-benefit plans, where you can be sure of a particular benefit. The benefit due to you upon retirement depends on the amount of money in the account and the payout method you select.

A **defined-benefit plan** is a traditional pension plan that promises you a specific level of payment upon retirement. The employer pays money into a fund, whose contributions and investment gains are used to pay the retirement benefit. Benefits accrue to you based on total years of participation in the plan and, usually, your final salary or your average salary for the last several years of your employment. As long as the plan is adequately funded, your benefit is guaranteed even if the plan's investments do poorly.

Some employers offer both types of pensions to their employees.

Vesting You are not entitled to pension benefits until your rights to the benefits have vested. **Vesting** refers to a point in time after which your accrued benefits cannot be taken away. Once you reach that point, you are entitled to be paid upon your retirement even if you subsequently leave your job.

ERISA prohibits your employer from firing you to avoid making benefit payments or to prevent benefits from vesting. However, you can lose nonvested benefits if you are fired for other reasons or if you quit.

ERISA provides two different methods for vesting. One method makes you eligible for 100 percent of your retirement benefit after five years of service. A second method provides for a graduated system of vesting. After three years of service you are eligible for 20 percent of your pension benefit; after four years, 40 percent; after five years, 60 percent; after six years, 80 percent; and after seven years, 100 percent.

If you also contribute to your pension plan from your own salary, your contributions always vest immediately, even if you haven't worked long enough to vest in contributions made by your employer. In other words, if you leave the company before your pension vests, you lose any benefits from your employer that you accrued under that plan, but you don't lose the money that you put in.

Because of vesting, you may be entitled to collect several pensions. As long as you worked in each of a series of jobs long enough for pension benefits to vest, you could receive a pension from each employer when you reach **retirement age** (defined in most pension plans as age 65, but many plans give you the option of retiring earlier—say beginning at 55 or 60—usually with reduced benefits).

How do you get your vested benefits when you leave your job? You have several options. You can get the vested funds as a lump-sum payment. However, if you get the money that way, you'll probably have to pay income tax on it at the time you receive payment. You can delay (and possibly lessen) the tax consequences by **rolling over** (quickly transferring) the money into an **Individual Retirement Account (IRA)** or another qualified pension plan, perhaps with your new employer.

Breaks in Service If a break in service occurs before benefits become vested, you lose any entitlement to them. A **break in service** occurs

---

PRESERVING PENSION RIGHTS
WHILE IN THE SERVICE

For obvious reasons, Congress wants to preserve your pension rights while you're serving your country. Under the **USERRA,** the time during which you were absent because of uniformed service must be counted as work with the employer for purposes of pension vesting and benefit accrual. Your employer is liable for funding the resulting pension obligation. However, if your employer's liability to make contributions to a pension fund is based on matching your contribution, the employer's funding obligation does not kick in until your matching contribution is made. If your plan *requires* contributions from you, you must be given an opportunity to make up for any contributions missed due to your military obligations upon return to work.

when employment is interrupted. When you work fewer than 500 hours in a year, a break in service has occurred; thus, layoffs and unpaid leaves can cause a break in service. However, leave for military service does not constitute a break in service (see box on the effect of the USERRA on pensions, p. 132).

Funding ERISA's funding requirements obligate the employer (and the employee, depending on the type of pension plan) to contribute enough money to cover pension payments when they become due, as determined actuarially. This part of the law aims to strengthen pension funds and prevent abuses. The employer and the fund's administrators are obligated to ensure that the funding requirements are met.

Administration of Funds ERISA also contains rules aimed at preventing misuse of pension funds. Those who manage pension funds are considered to be **fiduciaries** who are obligated to act with "care, skill, prudence, and diligence" in conducting the affairs of the pension plan. This means that the assets of the pension plan must be diversified among a group of investments so as to minimize the risk of large losses. Plan administrators are prohibited from using pension assets to invest in funds or property in which they have a financial interest, and from borrowing money from the fund for personal use or for making loans to the employer. If you're a pension plan participant, you have the right to sue administrators who breach their fiduciary duty.

Joint and Survivor Provisions This part of the law affects you if you are married. If you're single, you'll most likely receive a monthly pension for the rest of your life. (Some funds let you receive a lump sum, but that might have tax consequences, which you might delay or lessen by rolling it over to your IRA.)

If you're married and die before retirement, you could provide under the terms of the pension plan that all of your vested benefits be paid to your spouse. By law, the surviving spouse is entitled to a qualified preretirement survivor annuity, which generally provides that the spouse receive at least 50 percent of the amount of the vested benefits. (In effect this entitlement prevents a spouse from totally disinheriting the surviving spouse.) The survivor's benefit is automatically provided *unless* your spouse consents in writing to waive it.

ERISA also requires that a plan pay regular retirement benefits to your spouse when you die after beginning to receive retirement benefits. This is called the **qualified joint and survivor annuity benefit.** Under this benefit, your monthly check is reduced to leave something for your surviving spouse. When you die, he or she must receive a pension equal to at least 50 percent of the reduced pension. It is automatically provided under the pension plan *unless* your spouse consents in writing to waive the benefit.

Whether a divorced spouse is entitled to a share of your pension benefits depends on state law. Most states consider a pension to belong jointly to the worker and the worker's spouse. Even though it may have been earned by one member of the couple, it probably belongs to both. If a state court orders that part of your vested benefits be paid to an ex-spouse, ERISA requires the plan administrator to honor the court decree.

Terminating a Plan ERISA does not prevent your employer from ending its pension plan, but it does provide some protection for you if it does. If your employer voluntarily terminates its plan, it must notify both the plan participants and the **Pension Benefit Guaranty Corporation** (**PBGC**—a federal agency established by ERISA) of its intent to terminate. There must be sufficient assets in the plan to meet all benefit liabilities at the time of termination. The pension plan must first pay out to plan participants all benefits due under the pension plan. Any excess assets may revert to the employer, but such reversions are subject to a high excise tax to be paid by the employer.

ERISA also requires defined-benefit pension plans to pay insurance to the PBGC. In return, the PBGC guarantees the vested benefits of participants if a plan is terminated, up to a certain limit. The PBGC provides this protection only for certain benefits in specific types of funds. Not covered are plans of professional firms with 25 or fewer employees; plans paid for by union dues only; plans run by religious groups; and certain plans for company executives. It also may not protect benefits if you don't participate in a defined-benefit plan, benefits above a certain dollar amount, and benefits that are not vested. Some early retirement benefits are not covered, and if the plan provides medical and disability benefits, these too may not be covered.

Reporting and Disclosure Since each pension plan is different, it is important for you to know the specific terms of your plan. ERISA requires the employer to give a **summary plan description (SPD)** and a summary of the annual financial report to every participant in the pension plan. The SPD is a nontechnical explanation of how the plan works and how benefits are paid out. It explains the benefit accrual rules, vesting requirements and procedures for filing a claim for benefits. The summary of the annual financial report is a nontechnical explanation of the financial data relevant to the operation of the plan. ERISA also requires that employers make available to the plan participants, upon request, copies of the plan itself and the annual report.

FILING A CLAIM FOR YOUR PENSION

Filing a claim for pension benefits varies depending on the specific terms of the plan. Generally, if you're vested you're eligible for payments from your fund when you reach the age of 65 (or the normal retirement age specified in the plan). Most pension plans require you to file a written claim in order for payments to begin. Within 90 days, the plan administrators must either begin payment to you or notify you in writing that the claim is denied.

If a claim is denied, you are entitled to request a review of the decision. If, upon review, the claim is still denied, you can appeal that decision. Some plans provide for **arbitration** as the means of appeal. (In arbitration, a dispute is heard and resolved by a private individual or panel; it's an alternative to the formal court system.) When arbitration is required, you must use that mechanism. You can eventually challenge the denial of a claim in court by filing a lawsuit under ERISA.

SOCIAL SECURITY

Not every employee has a private pension plan, but almost all are entitled to social security old age benefits. Your social security benefit is in addition to your pension benefit, though in some private pension plans your benefits are reduced to take into account what you're receiving from social security. Almost every worker who has received credit for ten years of work is fully insured for retirement purposes under the social security laws. (Exceptions are some government workers and railroad workers.) Unlike a private pension plan, where you will lose any accrued benefits that have not vested if you change employers or have a break in service, social security benefits are not tied to any specific employer or consecutive years of service. Thus, you get credit toward the ten years of work regardless of how many employers you've worked for. Also, if you work for one year, are out of the workforce for two years, and then resume working, the initial one year of work will count toward the ten years of credit.

However, it's not enough just to work. You have to earn a minimum amount to get credit for benefits. For example, in 1996 you had to earn at least $640 in a quarter to receive credit for one-quarter year of work.

You are eligible for full retirement benefits at the **normal retirement age.** In 1997, the normal retirement age is 65; beginning in 2000, it will gradually be raised to 67 over a period of many years. You can get partial benefits at age 62. Conversely, if you delay retirement beyond the normal retirement age, your benefits will be higher when you finally do retire. The amount of money that you'll receive upon retirement depends on how much money you earned over your lifetime, and your age at retirement.

What if you want to work *and* receive benefits? If you are under age 70 and receiving benefits, you may earn only a certain amount of wages before your social security payments are reduced.

To receive social security retirement benefits, you must file a written application with the Social Security Administration. You should file two or three months before your retirement date. Your first check should arrive soon after you quit working.

DO SOME CHECKING BEFORE YOU RETIRE

To plan for your retirement, you'll want to know what benefits you'll be entitled to when you retire at a given age. Many employers provide such information routinely for their pension plans.

To get this information for your social security benefit any time before retirement, even years before, and to obtain an estimate of your benefit, just pick up a **Personal Earnings and Benefit Statement Form** at your local Social Security Administration office, or call toll-free at (800) 772-1213.

This statement not only estimates your benefits, but also tells you how much you have paid in and provides information so that you can make sure your employers have been depositing your share and theirs of the social security tax. If your wages were wrongly reported, you have three years from when the wages were earned to correct the mistake. However, there is no time limit on correcting an error caused by an employer's failure to report your earnings. You'll need proof, such as a pay stub, a written statement from the employer, or **Form OAR-7008 (Request for Correction of Earnings Record)**.

■

CHAPTER SIX

Unions in the Workplace

Rights for Both Workers and Employers

The **National Labor Relations Act** (**NLRA,** or the **Wagner Act**) is a federal law that governs union activity. It grants employees the right to engage in "concerted activity" (which includes union activity) free from employer interference, restraint and coercion. It establishes procedures for determining when the employees have chosen a union to represent them, and it regulates the relationship between unions and management in dealing with workplace issues.

The NLRA is based on the premise that individual employees have very little leverage in bargaining with their employer over wages, terms of employment and workplace problems. In practice, the employer unilaterally determines these issues without much discussion with workers. If, however, the workers pool their individual bargaining power and deal with the employer as a group, usually with the union acting as their representative, they can more effectively influence workplace conditions and resolve workplace problems.

If employers are covered under federal law, the NLRA generally preempts state regulation of their union-management relations. Most states, however, have passed laws closely modeled on the NLRA to regulate private sector employers exempt from federal law. The discussion that follows, therefore, will provide some insight into state law as well as the NLRA.

EMPLOYEE RIGHTS UNDER THE NLRA

The NLRA gives employees the right to:

- form and join unions;
- support and assist unions;
- choose a union to represent them for purposes of collective bargaining with their employer; and
- engage in group conduct that has as its purpose collective bargaining or helping each other regarding workplace issues.

The law also gives employees the right to choose *not* to engage in these activities.

Having given employees these rights, the law then protects them in exercising the rights. It prohibits both employers and unions from interfering with employees who are trying to engage in any of these activities.

The rights granted under the NLRA are not absolute. First, the rights are only given to "employees" who work for an employer covered by the NLRA. The NLRA regulates only private sector employers engaged in interstate commerce, excluding railroads and airlines. And certain categories of workers are not considered to be "employees" even if they work for a covered employer. These excluded workers are: domestic employees, farmworkers, independent contractors, supervisors, and managers. A **supervisor** is someone with authority to hire, fire, discipline, promote, or adjust the grievances of other employees or to effectively recommend to the company that such action be taken. A **manager** is a high-level employee who uses independent judgment in making and carrying out company policies.

Second, even if you are an "employee," you can lose the protection of the statute if you try to exercise your rights for an unlawful purpose or in a way that unnecessarily interferes with a legitimate employer interest.

WHAT EMPLOYEES CAN DO

We can't provide an exhaustive catalogue of employee activities protected by the NLRA, but the next few pages discuss the most common forms of protected activity.

The **right to form and join unions** includes the right to talk with union organizers and supporters, socialize with union organizers, attend union meetings, and obviously to sign up and become a member of a union. Forming a union often involves engaging in organizing activity. This activity includes discussing the benefits and disadvantages of unionization with other employees, soliciting employee signatures on **union authorization cards** (cards that authorize a union to act as bargaining representative for employees), distributing union literature, serving on a union organizing committee, and

---

ACTING TOGETHER WITHOUT A UNION

The right to engage in group conduct to help each other regarding workplace issues (**concerted activity**) is not limited to when a union is present. Employees have the right to engage in concerted activities even in the absence of a union. Employee activity in the absence of a union is protected concerted activity if it involves issues relating to workplace concerns and if there is **group conduct.**

Activity relates to workplace concerns when its purpose is to improve wages, benefits or conditions of work. There is obviously "group" conduct when two or more employees act together, but even action by an individual employee can sometimes be group action when that person is speaking on behalf of fellow employees. For example, one worker asking the employer to provide her with health insurance coverage is not engaged in protected concerted activity. If, however, the worker is acting as the spokesperson for other employees, or the employees go as a group to ask the employer for health insurance coverage, then both the worker and the individuals in the group would be protected.

---

wearing union insignia. Support and assistance to a union can take many forms: circulating or signing a petition in support of a union; engaging in a work stoppage in support of a union position; picketing and distributing handbills; contributing money; and speaking to other employees advocating the union's position.

Employees have the right to select the union that they want to represent them for bargaining, to change their representative from one union to another, and to change the composition of the union leadership. The decision whether or not to be represented by a union at all belongs to the employees. The employer and union can campaign for the support and votes of the employees, but the employees choose whether they will be represented.

Employees have the right to strike, to picket and distribute handbills in support of the union's bargaining demands, and to advocate in a variety of ways their support for the union's bargaining position.

The NLRA also guarantees employees the right to refrain from engaging in any activities. If you do not wish to participate in union activity, distribute handbills or strike, or don't want to participate in "group" conduct, you can't be required to do so.

WHAT EMPLOYEES CAN'T DO

As indicated above, these rights are not absolute. If the purpose or method of the employees' activity is illegal, or if the method unduly interferes with a legitimate employer interest, the activity will not be protected. Suppose a group of male workers complains to the employer because it promoted a woman to a supervisory position. They don't like working for a woman and ask the employer to demote the woman. This activity is not protected because they're trying to persuade the employer to discriminate based on sex, which violates Title VII.

Even if the objective is lawful, the way the employees conduct themselves may remove them from the protection of the law. For example, employees go on strike to get the employer to grant a wage increase, but in connection with the strike they vandalize the employer's property. Although the object of the strike (a wage increase) is lawful, the activity in connection with the strike (vandalism) is unprotected because it is unlawful and interferes with a legitimate employer property interest.

WHAT EMPLOYERS CAN AND CAN'T DO

When employees exercise rights protected under the NLRA, the employer can't interfere with their ability to engage in such conduct. It also can't discriminate against them in hiring, firing, and terms and conditions of employment because they have engaged in such conduct.

Employers might try to interfere with their employees' rights both by words and actions. The NLRA prohibits employers from threatening employees with adverse employment consequences because they have exercised, or may exercise, their rights. It's against the law for employers to threaten employees with loss of their jobs or benefits, to threaten discipline or reduction of hours, or to threaten plant shutdown if employees join a union.

Employers also can't "bribe" employees with promises. An employer promising employees a pay increase in return for voting against the union has violated the law. Questioning employees about their union sympathies or activities, or other types of protected activities, is also prohibited. Spying on employees as they engage in protected activity also constitutes unlawful interference.

Employer rules that unnecessarily interfere with the ability of employees to exercise their rights at the workplace also violate the law. Employees have the right to discuss union or workplace issues (**solicitation**), and to hand out leaflets or other printed material (**distribution**). Employers, on the other hand, have a legitimate interest in ensuring productivity in the workplace. To accommodate these competing interests, certain types of rules are allowed; others are prohibited.

Employers may make and uniformly enforce rules that prohibit solicitation during working time. **Working time** means the time employees are being paid to work; it does not include all time at the workplace. Thus, an employer may not prevent employees from discussing union issues during break times and mealtimes or before and after work. There is, however, an exception for retail businesses and hospitals: an employer may prohibit solicitation at any time on the selling floor and in immediate patient care areas.

Also, any such rule must be *uniformly* enforced. If the employer forbids only union discussion, permitting employees to sell Girl Scout cookies or solicit contributions for and talk about other causes during work time, the employer has violated the law.

The rationale behind allowing the employer to prohibit solicitation during work time is that the employer has a legitimate interest in getting a decent day's work for a decent day's pay. Allowing it to restrict solicitation may have the effect of restricting union activity (that is otherwise specifically protected under federal law), but the law attempts to balance both employer and union interests. For example, allowing employees to talk during work will interfere with their productivity. However, if the employer allows other types of solicitation during work time, then it is not concerned with productivity, and any restriction on union activity is not to further its legitimate business interests but rather to interfere with employees' rights.

The law allows the employer to regulate distribution of literature a little more broadly. Solicitation deals with the spoken word and infringes upon the employer's interests only to the extent that it occurs on working time. But distribution of literature, because it carries the potential of littering the employer's premises, raises a hazard to production whether it occurs on working time or nonworking time. Thus, an employer may prohibit distributing literature in work areas at all times. However, it must still allow distribution in nonwork areas, such as cafeterias and locker rooms. As with solicitation, any rules regulating distribution must be uniformly enforced.

The rules about solicitation and distribution at work apply only to employees. The employer can generally close its property to nonemployees, even if their purpose is to solicit employees on behalf of a union. Such a trespass rule must, of course, be uniformly enforced against all outside solicitors.

If a union has no other reasonable means of reaching employees—

say at a remote lumber camp or an oil rig—employers may have to allow nonemployee organizers onto the property.

The NLRA also prohibits an employer from taking **adverse employment actions** against employees because they have participated in conduct protected by the law. That means employers can't fire, demote, lay off, or refuse to hire you, or deny you a raise, because you have supported a union or engaged in other protected group activity. Just as an employer cannot threaten to fire you because you have joined a union, the employer also cannot carry out such a threat and actually fire you for that reason.

The fact that you have engaged in protected conduct does not, however, insulate you from discipline or discharge for other reasons. Employees who support a union may lawfully be disciplined for tardiness, absenteeism, poor performance or insubordination, *provided* that employees who do not support a union are similarly disciplined. As with antidiscrimination laws, the key is to treat similarly situated employees the same. If employees who exercise their rights under the NLRA are singled out for different treatment, the employer has violated the law.

How do you determine whether an employer took action against an employee because of protected activity? Courts ask:

SHOWING YOUR COLORS AT WORK

Employees often wear union T-shirts, buttons, or other insignia to show their support for the union. This is protected conduct under the law. Having a dress code or requiring uniforms isn't enough to justify a ban on insignia. In certain situations, however, the employer may be able to justify a regulation based on a legitimate business interest. For example, to prevent alienation of customers (where employees come in contact with customers) or to prevent adverse effects on patients in health care institutions, an employer may create some limits. While a total ban may not be justified, the employer could ban all but "tasteful and inconspicuous" insignia.

- Did the employer know that the employee engaged in protected activity?

- Has the employer made any statements indicating hostility toward the rights given to employees under the NLRA?

- Has the employee been treated differently and is there no satisfactory explanation of the difference?

- Was the employer's adverse action close in time to the employee's union activity?

- Was the employer's action disproportionate to the offense that the employee is alleged to have committed?

- Has the employer given conflicting reasons for its actions?

WHAT UNIONS CAN'T DO

The NLRA also prohibits union conduct that coerces employees in the exercise of their rights. Like management, unions are prohibited from "bribing" employees. The most common examples of unlawful conduct by unions are: violence and threats of physical violence directed at employees; acts of vandalism directed at the employer's property when done in the presence of employees; mass picketing of an employer's premises; or following an employee who is a strikebreaker home from work.

UNION ELECTION PROCEDURES

A union organizing campaign can start either because employees have contacted a union or because the union on its own seeks to organize the workers.

The first step in an organizing campaign is to inform the employees of the benefits and advantages of union representation and determine whether the employees have any interest in having the union represent them in their dealings with the employer. Employees are invited to attend union meetings during their off-duty hours. Employees discuss among themselves at the workplace the pros and cons of unionization. They are given leaflets containing information about the union. At some point, union authorization cards are circulated, and the union asks employees to sign the cards if they are interested in having the union represent them. If at least 30 percent of the workers in a unit (see p. 115 for a discussion of bargaining units) sign the card, the union can ask the **National Labor Relations Board (NLRB)** to hold a secret ballot election so employees can vote on whether to have a union. It is possible for a union to be voluntarily recognized by an employer without having to go through a secret ballot election. The employer can agree to a card check, in which it looks at the union authorization cards and if 50 percent plus one of the employees in the unit have signed, the employer agrees to negotiate with the union as the representative of its employees. Usually, however, employers insist on an election.

The employer also has the opportunity to talk to its employees about the disadvantages of union representation. It has the right to express its views and opinions about unionization, and to present arguments and information in an attempt to persuade the employees not to vote for the union. What an employer does not have the right to do is threaten or coerce the employees or promise them benefits; indeed, any threats or promises violate the law.

The election is conducted by secret ballot—employees are given the opportunity to vote for union representation or against it. The election is generally held at the employer's place of business so that all the workers have the opportunity to cast a ballot. The election is conducted by the NLRB to ensure that it is fair and employees can freely decide whether they want a union.

If the union wins the election, it becomes the bargaining agent for the employees and negotiates a collective bargaining agreement with the employer. If the union loses the election, the status quo prevails.

There is also an election procedure for voting out a union that currently represents a group of workers. This is called a **decertification election**. The decertification process can be initiated only by employees; if any managerial or supervisory personnel are involved in supporting or assisting the decertification it is not valid. As mentioned previously, the decision about whether or not to have union representation is one for the employees only; any employer instigation or encouragement of the decertification process is prohibited interference with employee rights.

Employees initiate the decertification process by circulating a petition, asking those employees who are interested in voting out the union to sign their names. If at least 30 percent of the employees sign such a petition, it can then be filed with the NLRB. The NLRB will schedule a secret ballot election among employees, who will then have the opportunity to vote on whether or not to retain the union as their representative.

COLLECTIVE BARGAINING AGREEMENTS

When a union wins an election, it doesn't necessarily represent every worker employed by the company. The union election is held among those employees who are considered to have a "community of interest" at the workplace. These employees form a **bargaining unit—**

REPRESENTING EVERYBODY IN THE UNIT

Once selected, the union is the exclusive bargaining agent for all the employees in the bargaining unit. In effect, it represents all the bargaining-unit employees on all workplace issues. Instead of each individual employee trying to deal with the employer on a one-to-one basis to change or improve conditions at work or resolve problems, the bargaining power of the employees is pooled together and the union acts as the representative of that pooled bargaining power.

The union represents all employees in the bargaining unit, even those who did not vote for the union. This concept is based on the democratic majoritarian principle: as in national politics, a senator represents, and makes decisions affecting, all the people in the state, including those who did not vote or those who voted for other candidates.

the group of workers represented by the union. The union is the exclusive bargaining representative of all employees in the bargaining unit.

Employees have a community of interest where they share similar working conditions, jobs, hours of work and supervision. For example, employees who work on an assembly line probably do not have a community of interest with office workers, but salespersons in a department store would probably share a community of interest even though they worked in different departments and sell different types of goods.

With the authority to act as exclusive representative comes the obligation to use that authority in a fair and nondiscriminatory manner. Thus, the NLRA imposes a duty of fair representation on all unions, requiring them to act in the best interest of all the bargaining-unit employees. Decisions that the union makes in dealing with workplace issues cannot be arbitrary, discriminatory or in bad faith. Unions are, however, given a wide range of discretion in exercising their authority to deal on behalf of employees. As the Supreme Court has stated: "The complete satisfaction of all who are represented is hardly to be expected. A wide range of reasonableness must be allowed a [union] in serving the [employees] it represents, subject always to complete good faith and honesty of purpose in the exercise of its discretion."

For example, let's say that in discussions with the employer, the union has to make a decision whether to ask for more money to be paid in wages or to be put into the pension plan; the employer will not give money for both. The younger workers may want more wages now, but the older workers may be more concerned with pensions. Obviously, whatever decision the union makes will leave some group dissatisfied. As long as the decision is not arbitrary, discriminatory or in bad faith, the union has not violated its duty of fair representation. If the union chooses pensions because it thinks that a healthy pension plan is important, this is an allowable decision. If the union chooses pensions because most of the older workers supported the union, while the younger workers had campaigned against the union, then its decision could be held to be discriminatory and in bad faith.

COLLECTIVE BARGAINING

As the exclusive bargaining agent for the employees, the first important duty for a newly elected union is to attempt to negotiate a collective bargaining agreement with the employer. The NLRA requires both the employer and the union to bargain in good faith with regard to wages, hours, and terms and conditions of employment for purposes of reaching an agreement. A refusal to bargain in good faith violates the law.

Imposing a duty on the employer to bargain in good faith means that once the union has been elected, the employer loses its ability to make unilateral decisions regarding wages, hours, and terms and conditions of employment. Before any changes can be made in the workplace that would affect these issues, the employer must bargain with the union and try to reach an agreement on the issue. For example, after a union wins an election, the employer wants to institute a new work rule banning smoking in the workplace. Unlike the situation before the union arrived when the employer could just go ahead and announce such a rule, the employer must now notify the union that it wants to impose the rule, and sit down and bargain in good faith with the union about the problem of smoking in the workplace and whether a rule is needed and, if so, what the rule should be.

Sometimes, however, the employer and the union are unable to agree on how to deal with an issue. They have negotiated in good faith but are unable to agree—they have reached an impasse. At this point the employer is allowed to put into effect the last proposal that it made to the union.

The fact that the union is the exclusive representative of the employees for purposes of bargaining means not only that the employer has the duty to bargain with that union, but that the employer is forbidden to negotiate with anyone else. The employer cannot negotiate workplace issues directly with the employees or with other unions.

Instead of bargaining over workplace issues as they arise, one at a time, unions and management usually negotiate a **collective bargaining agreement** that sets out the terms and conditions of employment. The collective bargaining agreement basically reduces to writing the "law of the shop." The employer and union usually agree on the benefits, duties and rules that will govern the relationship between the workers and the company for a set period of time. Most collective bargaining agreements are three years in length. The collective bargaining agreement is an enforceable contract binding on the employer, the union and the bargaining-unit employees.

In negotiating a collective bargaining agreement, the employer and union are obligated to discuss and try to reach agreement on **mandatory subjects**—all issues that relate to wages, hours, and terms and conditions of employment. Examples of items that fall within this description are: rates of pay, hours of work, health insurance, pension benefits, vacations, seniority rights, job assignments, work rules, and procedures for promotions, layoffs, recalls and transfers. The *duty* to bargain does not apply, however, to issues that do not involve wages, hours, and terms and conditions of employment—such as what types of products the company will manufacture or how much money to spend on advertising. Bargaining may get into these other areas and often does. However, the employer retains its unilateral decision-making authority on these issues even if it begins to bargain on them. If agreement is not reached, it can pull them off the table unilaterally and refuse to bargain further. However, once the union and employer come to terms on these issues, the employer is bound by the collective bargaining agreement.

Three provisions are found in almost all collective bargaining agreements: "just cause" clauses, grievance and arbitration clauses, and union security clauses.

- **Just Cause Clauses.** A **just cause clause** limits the employer's ability to discipline and fire employees. Unlike the employment at will situation, where the employer is free to discipline and discharge for good reasons, bad reasons or no reason at all, the just cause clause in a union contract requires that the employer have just cause (or **proper cause**) before disciplining or firing.

The just cause requirement limits not only the reasons for discipline, but also the types of discipline that can be imposed. Just cause usually requires that the reason for discipline be related to legitimate work issues. For example, it could be just cause to discipline an employee for absenteeism but not because an employee is a pro-choice advocate. (In an employment at will situation, the employer could discipline for either reason.) Just cause also requires that the "punishment fit the crime": firing an employee who is three minutes late to work would most likely be considered too severe and therefore not just cause. (Once again, in employment at will the employer would be free to fire the employee for that reason.)

Several factors help determine whether an employer's disciplinary action is for just cause:

- the company notified employees that the conduct in question could be cause for discipline;
- the rule is reasonably related to the efficient operation of the business;
- the employer undertook a fair and impartial investigation prior to imposing discipline and had reason to believe the employee committed the violation;
- the rule has been applied uniformly; and
- the discipline is not disproportionate to the offense involved and took into account the past record of the employee.

• **Grievance and Arbitration.** The grievance and arbitration provision of a collective bargaining agreement is the usual way of enforcing the terms of the contract. If employees or the union believe that the employer has violated the contract, they can file a complaint through the grievance procedure. The **grievance procedure** is usually a multistep process. Through it the union and the company attempt to resolve their dispute over the terms of the contract. If they cannot reach an agreement between themselves, the dispute is normally submitted to an arbitrator for decision.

The **arbitrator** is a neutral third party (an individual, a panel, or in some industries a joint committee of labor and management). The arbitrator holds a hearing at which both the union and employer present evidence and testimony in support of their interpretation of the contract provision in dispute. After considering the evidence, the arbitrator issues a decision stating which party's interpretation is correct. This decision is generally final and binding on the union and the company.

Not every grievance goes to arbitration. Many times the company and union agree on how to resolve the problem. Other times the union, after reviewing the situation, believes the employer acted correctly and did not violate the contract. Sometimes the union may think that it does not have a strong enough case to win at arbitration, even though it still thinks the employer is wrong.

Just because an employee files a grievance does not mean that the

---

A TYPICAL GRIEVANCE

Here is an example of how the grievance and arbitration process works. A collective bargaining agreement has a clause that states that where skill and experience are equal, the person with the most seniority gets the promotion. The employer awards a promotion to Employee Jones; Employee Smith has more seniority and thinks she is as good a worker as Jones so she should have gotten the promotion. Smith notifies the union that she thinks the employer violated the contract. This is usually done by filing a written grievance and giving it to the union shop steward. The shop steward notifies the company of the grievance and sets up a meeting to discuss the issue with a supervisor. If the steward and supervisor cannot agree on how to resolve this problem, then individuals higher up within the organizational structure (such as the business agent or union president and the plant manager) will discuss the issue. If they cannot agree, the case would be submitted to an arbitrator for decision.

union must pursue it through the grievance and arbitration process. As long as the union does not act arbitrarily, discriminatorily or in bad faith in deciding how to handle an employee's grievance, it has fulfilled its duty of fair representation. If the union decides not to pursue Employee Smith's grievance (see box on prior page) because it does not agree that she is equally as skilled as Jones, it has acted lawfully; if, however, the decision is based on the fact that Smith is a woman and Jones is a man, it has violated its duty of fair representation.

- **Union Security Clauses.** A **union security clause** requires *all* workers in the bargaining unit to make periodic payments to the union. Union members are required to pay certain dues and fees. The other employees in the bargaining unit are not required to join the union, but they can be required to pay for the work that the union performs on their behalf in negotiating and administering the collective bargaining agreement. These are called **service fees** or **fair share payments.** An employee who refuses to pay the required dues, fees, or payments can be fired. In effect, this is the workplace equivalent of taxes that we pay to support the operation of the government. We may not like the government's policies and may not have voted for the current leaders, but we are still required to pay taxes to support the work performed by the government on our behalf.

Union security clauses don't apply in three cases. First, about 20 states (mostly in the South and western mountain regions) by law can and do prohibit including union security clauses in collective bargaining agreements. Second, individuals whose religious beliefs prohibit them from supporting labor unions are exempt from paying the money to the union, but they can be required to pay an amount equivalent to the union dues and fees to a nonreligious, nonlabor charitable organization. This accommodation to an employee's religious beliefs is required under both the NLRA and Title VII. Third, individuals can object to paying any dues and fees that are spent for purposes unrelated to collective bargaining and representing the workforce. Objecting individuals must notify the union of their objection. In such a situation, they are entitled to have the amount of money they are required to pay reduced. If 20 percent of dues money went to support political candidates, they could have their union dues (or service fee or fair share payment) reduced by 20 percent.

STRIKES

The NLRA specifically protects employees' right to strike. But, as with other rights contained in this law, the right to strike is not absolute. Some restrictions apply.

The protected nature of a strike depends on the object or purpose of the strike, the conduct of the strikers and the timing of the strike.

• **The Strike's Purpose.** If workers strike to obtain economic benefits and improved terms and conditions of employment, or to support union bargaining demands, the strike is an **economic strike.** Economic strikes are lawful. Economic strikers retain their status as employees, and firing them for striking violates the NLRA. The employer does have the right, however, to hire replacement workers to continue its operation. If the employer has hired permanent replacements, striking workers whose jobs have been filled by permanent replacement workers will not be entitled to their jobs when the strike ends. The striking employee does have the right to be recalled to the first vacancy that later occurs, whether because a replacement worker resigns or is fired, or the employer expands its business. Refusing to recall the economic striker to the first substantially equivalent job vacancy violates the law.

If the employer has hired only temporary replacement workers during the economic strike, then striking workers have a right to get their jobs back as soon as the strike ends. Whether a replacement worker is permanent or temporary depends on what the employer told the replacement worker at the time he or she was hired. If workers are told that they are being hired only until the strike is over, they are temporary replacements; if they were told that they have the job regardless of the strike ending, they are permanent replacements.

If the object of the strike is to protest unfair labor practices committed by the employer, the strike is an **unfair labor practice strike.** Unfair labor practice strikes are not only lawful, but offer more protection to strikers. They cannot be permanently replaced and have the right to be immediately reinstated upon their unconditional offer to return to work. An employer that refuses to reinstate unfair labor practice strikers violates the NLRA.

Sympathy strikers are workers who are not directly involved in the labor dispute, but rather are acting in solidarity with striking workers. As long as the strike itself is lawful, sympathy strikers are engaged in protected conduct and cannot be fired or disciplined.

Sympathy strikers who support a strike by another group of employees against a common employer are entitled to the same reinstatement rights as the strikers themselves. For example, the assembly line workers at a manufacturing plant strike to support their bargaining demands. The manufacturing plant clerical workers, who are not part of the bargaining unit and are not represented by a union, refuse to cross the picket line. The clerical workers are sympathy strikers against a common employer. Employees who refuse to cross an economic picket line have the same reinstatement rights as economic strikers; employees who refuse to cross an unfair labor practice picket line are entitled to the same reinstatement rights as unfair labor practice strikers.

Sympathy strikers can also support a strike of a group of workers employed by a *different* employer. For example, truck drivers are supposed to make a delivery to a manufacturing plant where the assembly line workers are on strike. When they see the picket line, they refuse to drive across it to make the delivery. They are sympathy strikers supporting a strike by workers employed by a different employer. They cannot be fired for refusing to cross the picket line, but they may be replaced. This is true whether the employees they are supporting are unfair labor practice strikers or economic strikers.

• **Conduct of the Strikers.** Striking workers who engage in certain types of conduct during a strike are unprotected and can be disciplined or fired. Threats of force or actual violence committed by striking workers is unprotected conduct. Vandalism and sabotage of the employer's property are also unprotected. Only strikers who actually engage in the unprotected conduct can lawfully be punished; not all striking workers are responsible.

Sit-down strikes and intermittent strikes are also unprotected. A **sit-down strike** is when striking workers refuse to leave the employer's property. An example of an **intermittent strike** is when employees engage in a five-hour work stoppage one day, then two days later engage in another five-hour strike, and then two days later do it again.

• **Timing of the Strike.** Many collective bargaining agreements contain **no-strike clauses.** Under these clauses the workers agree that for the contract's duration they will not strike. If they go out on strike in breach of a no-strike clause, they are unprotected and the employer can discipline or fire them.

The NLRA requires workers who are employed by health care institutions to give ten days' notice before they go on strike. If they fail to give the notice or go out on strike before the ten-day period runs, they are not protected and can lawfully be disciplined or fired.

SECONDARY BOYCOTTS OUTLAWED

Secondary boycotts are illegal under the NLRA. A **secondary boycott** is picketing aimed at a company the union does not have a dispute with (**secondary employer**), but which does business with an employer with whom the union does have a dispute (**primary employer**). Its purpose is to put pressure on the secondary employer to cease doing business with the primary employer. For example, truck drivers are engaged in an economic strike against Acme Trucking Company, their employer. Beta Manufacturing Company has a contract with Acme to deliver material and supplies to its factory. The truck drivers picket Beta Manufacturing Company—this is an illegal secondary boycott.

HIRING HALLS

Hiring halls are basically union-run employment agencies. They are prevalent in the construction and maritime industries, and to some extent are used in the trucking industry. The employers in these industries tend to be mobile, and employment is often short-term or irregular, making conventional hiring methods inefficient. In some circumstances, therefore, the unions whose membership is composed of workers in these industries operate hiring halls that function as employment clearinghouses. Employees who are available for work register at the hiring hall. Employers contact the hall and request a specific number of workers for a certain job. The union dispatches the registered workers. The employer and union may formalize this arrangement in a collective bargaining agreement, or it may just be an informal arrangement.

Whether by written agreement or practice, if the employer agrees to use the hiring hall as the exclusive means for hiring workers, it is called an **exclusive hiring hall.** If the employer merely uses the hiring hall as one source among many for recruiting workers, it is a **nonexclusive hiring hall.**

In an exclusive hiring hall arrangement, the union must allow any worker to register for referral, whether the individual is a union member or not. Refusing to allow nonunion workers to register violates the NLRA. Such workers may, however, be charged a fee for the use of the referral service. A union can refuse to allow nonmembers to use a nonexclusive hiring hall.

In referring workers from a hiring hall, whether it is exclusive or nonexclusive, the union must fulfill its duty of fair representation. Thus, it cannot decide which workers to refer based on arbitrary, discriminatory or bad faith reasons. A union that refers white workers before African-American workers, for instance, has acted in a prohibited discriminatory manner and violated its duty of fair representation. It has also violated Title VII, which prohibits labor unions from discriminating in referrals based on race.

INTERNAL UNION AFFAIRS

The **Labor-Management Reporting and Disclosure Act (LMRDA)**, (also known as the **Landrum-Griffin Act**) deals mainly with the relationship between unions and their members. The law grants union members certain basic political rights within the union organization:

- the right to free speech and assembly;
- the right to vote on union business and in union officer elections;
- the right to a secret ballot election before dues are increased;
- procedural safeguards against union discipline; and
- protection from retaliation for enforcing their rights.

The law also requires unions to file annual reports with the Department of Labor disclosing information about their fiscal operations. The law contains procedural requirements that must be satisfied as a condition of a national or international union imposing a trusteeship on a local union. A trusteeship occurs when a national union takes over the operations of a local union because the local officers have been involved in criminal activity or financial mismanagement.

THE RAILWAY LABOR ACT (RLA)

Most of the rights granted to employees under the RLA, as well as the restrictions imposed on employers and unions, are similar to those found in the NLRA. The enforcement procedures differ, of course, since different federal agencies were created to deal with the two laws. There are three major differences worthy of note, however.

First, secondary boycotts are not illegal under the RLA. Second, the law imposes a "cooling off" period after bargaining breaks down before a union can go on strike. Third, disputes over the application and interpretation of collective bargaining agreements are usually submitted to an Adjustment Board for resolution rather than to private arbitration.

The law also imposes requirements for ensuring fair election of union officers. Last, the law imposes fiduciary obligations on union officers to exercise their authority in the best interests of the union members and the union as a whole.

Unlike the NLRA, which grants rights to all employees, the LMRDA grants rights only to employees who have joined the union. An employee who is in a bargaining unit that is represented by a union, but who is not a member of that union, does not obtain any rights under the LMRDA.

CHAPTER SEVEN

■

Government Employment

Civil Service, Constitutional Protections, and Other Special Features

GOVERNMENT EMPLOYMENT IS DIFFERENT from private sector employment. By government workers, we mean people who work for the federal, state, or local government. Private sector workers are all nongovernmental employees. The law sometimes recognizes a distinction in how government workers are to be treated.

Many labor and employment laws apply to both government and private sector employers. In particular, all the antidiscrimination laws apply to both. There are a few notable exceptions: the **OSH Act, ERISA,** the **Employee Polygraph Protection Act,** and the **NLRA** do not apply to government employers. However, the exemption from the NLRA is counterbalanced by laws in most states dealing with union issues in government employment, and the federal government has also passed such a law dealing with its workers.

On the other hand, because government workers are employed by the government, they have additional protections not available to private sector employees. Civil service laws and rights guaranteed under the U.S. Constitution and state constitutions limit what government employers can do vis-à-vis their employees.

GOVERNMENT LABOR-MANAGEMENT RELATIONS

Both the **Federal Labor Relations Act (FLRA)** and the various state government labor relations laws draw heavily on the legal principles established under the NLRA. In fact, the FLRA and many state laws incorporate various sections of the NLRA verbatim. Many of the protections, therefore, that were discussed in Chapter 6, dealing with unions in the workplace, apply to government employees.

There are, however, three major differences between the NLRA and the various government union laws.

First, the categories of workers covered by these laws are sometimes broader than under the NLRA. The NLRA exempts supervisory employees from its protection, but some states (such as Hawaii, Michigan and New York) include government supervisory employees within the protection of state laws. The FLRA, however, like the NLRA, expressly excludes supervisors.

Second, the workplace issues that are subject to negotiation with the union tend to be more limited in government employment. The NLRA broadly defines the subjects of bargaining as "wages, hours, terms and conditions of employment." Many state laws also define bargaining subjects using these terms, but then go on to prohibit bargaining over certain specific issues. Sometimes they prohibit bargaining on any issue relating to managerial prerogatives. For example, the school curriculum, length of the school day and scheduling of extracurricular activities may not be bargaining issues under some state teacher laws. Or issues that are already regulated under a state civil service or merit system law are often excluded from bargaining. The FLRA prohibits federal agencies from bargaining over wages, limiting the bargainable issues to "conditions of employment."

Third, the FLRA and many state laws prohibit government workers from going out on strike. A strike exerts pressure on an employer to agree to the employees' bargaining demands. Without the ability to strike, employees have no weapons to try to persuade a recalcitrant employer to change its bargaining position and agree to their proposals. Accordingly, laws that prohibit strikes also provide **impasse resolution procedures** as a means of helping the parties reach an agreement when they are deadlocked. These procedures range from mediation to fact-finding and arbitration. In some cases, if the employer and union are unable to agree to the terms of a contract, a third-party arbitrator will decide what the contract terms will be.

CIVIL SERVICE LAWS

Every state, as well as the federal government, has enacted **civil service laws.** These laws require that employment policies be based on merit. They try to eliminate political considerations in the government employment process. Civil service systems generally include guidelines for recruiting applicants, testing programs for screening applicants, impartial hiring criteria based on merit, job classifications based on duties and responsibilities, and protection against arbitrary discipline and discharge.

Not all jobs within the government are under civil service. Some types of jobs are exempt. For example, high-level policy-making positions are rarely covered under the civil service rules. Neither are jobs, such as legal work done by attorneys, that involve a high level of specialized skill for which examination would be difficult.

If you're hired under civil service and have completed a probationary period, you may usually be fired only for **good cause.** Generally, this requires that the firing be based on work-related considerations that promote the efficiency of government operations.

A commission is usually established to ensure that the government employer is following the civil service rules. This commission hears and decides employees' complaints that their rights under the civil service regulations have been violated. The particulars of civil service laws and the role and operation of the commission vary from state to state.

CONSTITUTIONAL PROTECTIONS

The rights guaranteed to individuals by the U.S. Constitution are guaranteed against *government* restrictions. Thus, the First Amendment provides that "Congress shall make no law . . . abridging the freedom of speech." If the government prevents an individual from speaking out, it may run afoul of the Constitution.

The Constitution does not place restraints on what *private* persons can do. A private sector employer who refuses to hire someone because that person is a member of the American Civil Liberties Union (ACLU) has not done anything prohibited by the Constitution. If a private company prevents an employee from speaking out, it probably won't violate the Constitution.

A government employer, since it is the government, is subject to the Constitution in its dealings with its employees. It could not refuse to hire the ACLU member; it might not be able to limit an employee's speech.

The Supreme Court has recognized, however, that when the government acts as an employer it may have special interests. Providing effective and efficient service may require certain restrictions on employees that the government could not impose on ordinary individuals. Government employees may thus be subjected to some employment rules that infringe on their constitutional rights.

Therefore, government employees have greater protection in certain instances than private sector employees, but do not enjoy the full protection of the Constitution that is available to the ordinary citizen.

FREEDOM OF SPEECH

Under the **First Amendment,** government workers are guaranteed the right to speak their mind, but at the same time the government employer needs to effectively perform its services. In order to accommodate these two competing interests, the Supreme Court has developed a balancing test for deciding the limits of employees' free speech rights. The courts "balance ... the interests of the [employee], as a citizen, in commenting upon matters of public concern and the interest of the State, as an employer, in promoting the efficiency of the public services it performs through its employees."

The first question concerns the content of the employee's speech—is it a matter of public concern or only a matter of purely personal interest? A schoolteacher criticizing the curriculum developed by the school board is speaking on a matter of public concern.

A teacher complaining about not getting a raise is speaking about a personal matter. Courts have held that employees' speech about public matters is entitled to First Amendment protection. Speech about purely private concerns is not.

If the speech involves public issues, the government employer could still try to prevent the speech or discipline the employee involved, but it must show that it reasonably believes that the speech might be disruptive and interfere with efficient government operations. In doing so, the manner, time and place of the employee's speech are relevant. For example, would the speech disrupt the workplace and interfere with getting work done?

These cases are decided individually, and obviously depend on the particulars of each situation. However, the Supreme Court has suggested certain factors to be looked at: "[P]ertinent considerations [are] whether the statement impairs discipline by superiors or harmony among coworkers, has a detrimental impact on close working relationships for which personal loyalty and confidence are necessary, or impedes the performance of the speaker's duties or interferes with the regular operation of the enterprise."

Without sufficient justification, the government can't discipline or fire government employees based on speech that involves matters of public concern.

FREEDOM OF ASSOCIATION

The **First Amendment** freedom to associate goes along with the First Amendment right to free speech. This means that individuals have the right to associate with other individuals or belong to groups and organizations (whether they be the Nation of Islam, the ACLU, or the Ku Klux Klan) without fear of government interference or retaliation. As with free speech rights, a government employer can't infringe on employees' freedom to associate without significant employment-related justification.

Generally, a government employer cannot ask applicants about membership in organizations or who their friends and acquaintances are. Nor can the employer justify not hiring someone, or taking other adverse action, because of membership in a group or other personal ties. The government can't take such ties into account unless they are substantially related to a legitimate government interest.

However, in a few situations restrictions on political activism are permitted. The government employer may make employment decisions based on political affiliation *if* the job in question is a high-level policy-making position requiring the employee to carry out the political agenda of elected officials. For example, cabinet members and their top assistants can be hired and fired based on their political affiliations. But secretaries and clerical and administrative employees, as well as professional-level employees without policy-making duties, can't be fired or disciplined because of their political affiliations.

The government may also restrict the political activities of employees, regardless of the job they have, to secure a politically neutral civil service. The federal government enacted the **Hatch Act** to restrict certain types of political activity by federal government employees. There are two basic prohibitions: employees cannot use their official authority to interfere with or affect the result of an election, and employees cannot take active leadership or organizational roles in partisan political management or campaigns. But employees can participate in politics as individuals, and can express opinions about political matters. Employees who violate the Hatch Act can be disciplined or fired.

States also regulate their employees' political activities. Many state laws duplicate the Hatch Act. A few are more restrictive, in that they prohibit both nonpartisan and partisan political activity. Some state laws are less restrictive, prohibiting political activity only during work hours or if it interferes with work duties.

EMPLOYEE SEARCHES

The **Fourth Amendment** prohibits the government from conducting unreasonable searches and seizures. In the employment context, this limits the government employer's drug testing of employees, as well as searches of employees' possessions.

• **Drug Testing.** Drug testing of government employees is generally allowed under two circumstances. First, if the government employer has a reasonable suspicion that an employee is involved in drug use, it can require the employee to undergo a drug test. **Reasonable suspicion** must normally be based on specific facts implying drug use and not assumptions or rumors.

Second, a test is allowed if the government employer has a **compelling interest** in requiring it. The courts have found compelling governmental interests in the following situations:

1. postaccident testing of transportation employees involved in serious accidents;
2. testing of employees involved in the war against drugs, such as customs agents;
3. testing of employees in positions requiring them to carry firearms;
4. testing of employees in positions with access to sensitive government information; and
5. testing of employees with duties that have an immediate impact on public safety.

• **Searches.** To receive the protection of the Fourth Amendment, the government employee must first have a **reasonable expectation of privacy** in the thing to be searched. A worker probably doesn't have a reasonable expectation of privacy in a desk or filing cabinet shared with coworkers, or a work area exposed to the public. The worker's expectation of privacy would obviously be much higher in a locked drawer in an unshared desk.

When the employee can establish such a reasonable expectation, the employer's ability to search is subject to some restrictions. As with an employee's right to freedom of speech, the right to be free of unreasonable searches must be balanced, according to the Supreme Court, against the "government's need for supervision, control and the efficient operation of the workplace." The general rule is that the government employer may conduct an investigatory search for work-related misconduct, as well as a work-related non-investigatory search, only if there are "reasonable grounds for suspecting that the employee is guilty of work-related misconduct, or that the search is necessary for a noninvestigatory work-related purpose such as to retrieve a needed file." Moreover, any search must be conducted in a manner that is "reasonably related to the objectives of the search and not excessively intrusive."

Although the law on this point is unsettled, government employers would likely need probable cause to suspect workplace misconduct before they could search personal items, such as a briefcase, luggage or a purse, that an employee brings into the workplace. **Probable cause** is a legal standard in search and seizure law, requiring facts sufficient to cause a reasonable person to believe that contraband is likely to be found in the area to be searched.

THE RIGHT AGAINST SELF-INCRIMINATION

The **Fifth Amendment** protects persons from being compelled to be a witness against themselves in a criminal case. Thus, government employees can refuse to answer their employer's questions when the answer might subject them to criminal prosecution. The privilege against incrimination applies, for example, if the government employer questions employees about illegal drug use, or asks if they received a bribe.

Since the Fifth Amendment protects against compulsion in these situations, the government employer could not threaten to fire an employee who refused to answer incriminating questions, nor could it refuse to hire such an employee.

If, however, a government employer grants employees immunity to criminal prosecution based on any information they disclose, employees can be required to answer the questions or face discipline or discharge.

It is important to note that this Fifth Amendment protection extends only to answers that would subject the employee to criminal liability. Thus, if a government employer questions employees about whether they were sleeping on the job, the employees can be required to answer.

THE RIGHT TO PRIVACY

The Supreme Court has interpreted the Constitution as granting to individuals a right to privacy against government intrusion. The Court, however, has narrowly defined the scope of this privacy right, limiting it to conduct related to traditional family concerns, such as marriage, child-rearing and abortion. Government employers, therefore, are prohibited from asking questions about, or basing employment decisions on, these fundamental privacy interests.

THE RIGHT TO DUE PROCESS

The **Fifth Amendment** prohibits the government from depriving an individual of liberty or property without due process. In the employment situation, discipline or discharge can, in some circumstances, constitute a deprivation of the employee's liberty or property interests. In such case, the government employer must provide due process before firing or disciplining. It is important to note, however, that not all discipline and discharge decisions involve liberty or property rights.

Government employees' liberty interests in their job are involved if:

1. the way employees are disciplined or dismissed impugns their character as the result of a false characterization; and
2. the stain on employees' character is made public.

In determining whether government employees have a **property interest** in their job, the courts look at whether there is a written or implied contract granting them a property interest in the job or if a statute gives them a property interest in the job. For example, teachers with tenure are considered to have a property interest in their job, because there is an express understanding that tenure means one cannot lose a job without just cause.

When liberty or property interests are at stake, the government must give the employee due process before taking away that interest. **Due process** requires that:

- employees be given notice of the reason for being discharged;
- a hearing be held at which employees are given the opportunity to present evidence in their behalf and to hear the evidence presented against them; and
- a decision be made by an impartial third-party decision-maker based on the evidence presented at the hearing.

CHAPTER EIGHT

■

Enforcing Workplace Rights

Guidelines for Resolving Workplace Problems

THERE IS NO SINGLE UNIFORM METHOD for enforcing the rights discussed in this book. Given the same set of facts, you could well have multiple avenues for enforcing a right.

Often you might go through private grievance and arbitration systems. Other times, you'll file a complaint with a government agency, which has the authority to investigate and prosecute violations of the law. Sometimes, you'll need to file a lawsuit in court. While you're technically not required to have a lawyer to do so, lawsuits are complicated, and the other side will probably be well represented by legal counsel. To have a real chance of winning, you probably need a lawyer. In many circumstances, you may be required to use a combination of these procedures to enforce your rights.

Generally, however, it's a good idea to first discuss any workplace problems directly with your employer. Only if such discussion proves futile does it make sense to involve a third party, whether that party is a government agency or a lawyer.

INTERNAL COMPLAINT PROCEDURES

Many companies have policies for bringing workplace issues to the employer's attention. These policies may be contained in company handbooks or manuals or posted on company bulletin boards, or may just be common knowledge in the shop. Following these procedures often results in a fast, easy and inexpensive resolution of the problem.

Even if the employer does not have an established procedure, it's a good idea to contact someone within the company to discuss the issues and obtain information. Your immediate supervisor or the company human-resources/personnel department is a logical starting point.

Before you actually meet with a company representative, it is a good idea to prepare for the meeting by briefly outlining what you

---

SETTLING DISPUTES AMICABLY

Mediation is another way of resolving workplace problems. When an employee and the employer's representative are unable to reach an agreement on how to deal with a problem by talking it out between the two of them, a neutral third party can help them work it out. This neutral third party (the **mediator**) does not provide an answer, but helps the parties arrive at their own mutually agreeable answer. The mediator can clarify the issues, alleviate tensions between the parties, and act as a sounding board for testing out possible solutions. The final resolution of the problem remains, at all times, with the employee and the employer's representative. But the help of this neutral third party is sometimes the catalyst that will produce a final resolution.

Many communities have local mediation centers that have a list of available and trained mediators. The American Arbitration Association has a list of mediators with experience in employment disputes and will assist the parties in appointing an acceptable mediator and scheduling a meeting. There are also private companies and individuals that offer mediation services and are listed in the telephone book. Some local mediation centers offer their services for free, but most mediators charge an hourly fee that varies based on the mediator. It is up to the company and the individual to determine how any fees will be paid—many times the parties split the fee, but sometimes a company will agree to pay the entire fee. When the parties are serious about trying to work out their problems and are prepared, many disputes can be resolved in one mediation session.

---

perceive to be the problem or issue you would like the company to address, and what solution(s) you are proposing to deal with the issue. Once you have this clearly in your own mind, you will be in a better position to clearly and directly present the information to the employer. Give the company's representative a chance to respond to your concerns and listen to their perspective on the issue. It is often a good idea to take notes during the discussion—this helps to keep you focused on the issues. Try to stay calm; being highly emotional may cloud your judgment and distract you from accomplishing your objective.

In some circumstances, employees can be required to use a dispute resolution process that has been set up by the company. As a general rule, in order for the courts to recognize the validity of decisions reached using these processes, they should involve the use of independent third parties who are not employed by, or controlled by, the company. In certain financial industries, like insurance companies, banks and brokerage firms, employees who sell securities are required to execute registration forms. These forms contain clauses that require the employee to submit any employment-related dispute to binding arbitration. Similar contracts are becoming common in other industries.

The courts have enforced these clauses and dismissed lawsuits that employees have filed, requiring them instead to use arbitration. As long as the employee and employer sign a written document agreeing to submit any employment-related disputes to arbitration, the courts will usually enforce the contract. Some courts will consider whether employees voluntarily signed the document, with knowledge that they were waiving their right to file a lawsuit in court. The **NLRB** and the **EEOC** both take the position that requiring an employee to sign an arbitration agreement preventing them from filing charges with the NLRB or the EEOC in order either to be hired or to continue on the job violates the employee's rights under the **NLRA** and **Title VII**. The courts have not yet ruled on this issue.

When employees attempt to enforce their right to a benefit found in a company personnel handbook or manual (the **implied contract** theory), courts may require them to use any grievance mechanism that is contained in that same handbook or manual. The rationale is that if you argue that the statements in the manual create a contract, then all the provisions in the manual are part of that contract. If you want the benefits of the manual, you are also bound by its other terms. The practical effect is that you may not be able to sue in court until all the internal grievance procedures are completed, or you may not be able to sue at all.

Similarly, employees who claim rights contained in collective bargaining agreements are also required to use these contracts' grievance mechanisms to enforce those rights. The overwhelming majority of collective bargaining agreements contain grievance-arbitration provisions for enforcing the contract rights. The grievance-arbitration procedure is described in the section on collective bargaining agreements in Chapter 6. In those rare collective bargaining agreements that do not have arbitration provisions, employees can file a lawsuit in court to enforce their rights.

ARBITRATION

In **arbitration** the parties submit their dispute to a neutral third party. Unlike a mediator, who helps the parties come up with their own solution, the arbitrator, like a judge, issues a decision resolving the dispute. The arbitrator presides over a hearing, during which both parties have the opportunity to present evidence and testimony supporting their position, and make arguments to the arbitrator as to why their position is the correct one.

After the hearing, the arbitrator issues a decision, stating which party won the case and what the remedy is. For example, if the dispute involves whether or not the employer had the right to fire someone, the arbitrator could decide that the employer acted within its rights and the employee is not entitled to a remedy. Or the arbitrator could decide that the employer was wrong and direct the employer to reinstate the worker with back pay to make up for lost wages, or may direct the employer to reinstate the worker without back pay.

The arbitration process is similar to a court hearing in that the parties have the opportunity to present their cases to a neutral third party who has the authority to decide the dispute and issue a remedy. There are some differences, however. The process is less formal than court, and it is usually cheaper and faster. But there may be less opportunity before the hearing to have access to all the relevant documents and to talk to all the witnesses. In some circumstances, the arbitrator may not give the full range of remedies that would be available from a court.

Generally speaking, the decision of the arbitrator is final and binding. If either party is dissatisfied with the decision, it can file an appeal with a court, but the scope of the court's review is very limited. Courts will not overturn the decision merely because they disagree with the arbitrator's findings of facts or legal conclusions. If, however, there was evident partiality or corruption in the arbitrator, or the decision was procured by corruption, fraud or undue means, or the arbitrator was guilty of misconduct that prejudiced the rights of a party, a court may overturn an arbitration decision.

WHEN DO YOU NEED A LAWYER?

Should you hire a lawyer in a workplace dispute? As usual, it depends. One factor is the process being used to deal with the dispute. Another is the stage of the process—you may not need a lawyer initially, but you might need one as the process gets more formal. A third is the size of the dispute. The more there is at stake, the more professional help makes sense.

Disputes that are still in the informal stages of resolution—discussions between the employer and employee or mediation—are probably best handled by the parties themselves. However, individuals who are uncomfortable with conflict, who feel at a disadvantage in expressing themselves or who are unsure as to their rights and obligations may want to consult an attorney even at this early stage in the process.

If the dispute is relatively minor and resolved amicably, neither side probably needs a lawyer to review the final settlement. But sometimes enough is at stake that it might be advisable to get a lawyer's approval of even a mediated settlement.

When government enforcement agencies become involved, it may be appropriate for an *employer* to retain an attorney. Enforcement agencies have the responsibility to ensure compliance with the law. When complaints are filed, they investigate and determine whether there is reason to believe the law has been violated. An attorney who understands the law and the investigation process can help to ensure that the government agency has access to the information necessary to understand the employer's conduct. A finding of no violation by the government may put the dispute to rest.

It is not quite as important for an *individual* to have an attorney at this stage. The agency personnel know the law and have been trained to uncover the facts necessary to determine if there is reason to believe a violation has occurred. However, hiring an attorney at this stage often makes sense. An attorney can help the employee organize and present the information to the agency, highlight the probable legal issues involved and suggest possible avenues of investigation. In effect the attorney provides a safety net to ensure that the agency does not overlook critical information or issues.

Once a dispute reaches the **adjudication stage** (a hearing held before a neutral third party), it is usually a good idea for all parties to be represented by an attorney. This applies even to hearings outside the formal court system, such as in arbitration or before an administrative agency, where an **administrative law judge (ALJ)** presides. (An ALJ presides over administrative hearings, administers oaths, rules on evidence, takes testimony, makes findings of fact, and recommends conclusions of law.)

All these hearings have rules and procedures. Presenting a case successfully requires knowledge of the law and the rules of the process. Third-party decision-makers (whether they are ALJs, arbitrators, or judges) rely on the parties to present all the evidence and arguments necessary for a decision. They don't independently investigate a case. A party can lose by failing to introduce an important piece of evidence or neglecting to inform the decision-maker of the relevant case law affecting the issue. In some administrative hearings, such as before the NLRB or OSHA, a government attorney will present the case on behalf of the employee who filed the complaint. The attorney represents the public interest, and not the individual employee per se, but often the two interests are the same and the individual may not find it necessary to have separate representation.

FINDING THE RIGHT LAWYER

It's a good idea to choose a lawyer who regularly handles labor and employment cases, since this is a complex and specialized area of law. How do you find one? It's helpful to get recommendations from other businesses, a union, or an acquaintance who has used a labor lawyer. Your state or local bar association may have a lawyer referral service that can steer you toward lawyers specializing in this area. Or you may meet the income eligibility guidelines for representation by a Legal Services lawyer.

Many lawyers are willing to meet with you briefly without charge so that the two of you can get acquinted. At (or soon after) this first meeting, you can decide whether you want to hire that lawyer. Before you make that decision, you might want to

- ask about the lawyer's experience and area of practice;
- ask who will be working on your case;
- ask about fees and costs (see below);
- ask about possible outcomes of the case;
- ask how you can participate (and possibly lower the cost to yourself).

If you've made a complaint in a **Title VII** case, you can ask the court to appoint an attorney to represent you. The court, however, cannot force an attorney to take the case; in effect the court makes a referral of the case to an attorney. Moreover, before the court will refer a case, it will consider your financial condition, the likelihood that you can win the case, and the efforts that you have made on your own to get an attorney.

ADMINISTRATIVE AGENCY PROCEDURES

What if you can't resolve the problem informally? You've tried to talk it out, maybe even tried mediation, but the two sides are still far apart.

The next step is usually going to the administrative agency—such as the Equal Employment Opportunity Commission or the National Labor Relations Board—that enforces the law that you think protects you. (See Appendix II for a full listing of laws, enforcing agencies, and steps to take to make a complaint.)

LAWYERS' FEES

If you're considering a lawyer, you're naturally concerned with fees. In employment cases, attorneys generally charge an hourly rate for their services. You'll want to discuss fees with each lawyer you interview, trying to get a feel for the likely range of fees you'll be charged, whether you will be billed at a lesser rate for associates and paralegals who work on the case, how long you have to pay fees, how you can help reduce them, and so on.

Many of the labor statutes provide for the award of attorney's fees to the plaintiff if he or she wins the case. This means that the defendant could be required to pay for your attorney.

Workers' compensation cases and state law tort claims are often handled for plaintiffs by lawyers who agree to a **contingency fee arrangement.** In contingency fee cases, the fee is a percentage of the money awarded to you if you win. The percentage is often one third, though it may be negotiable. If you lose, you'd be liable for costs—filing fees, fees for serving summonses, costs of postage, copying documents, expert witnesses, and so on—but not the lawyer's time.

This is preferable to going to court in several ways. For one thing, the laws are often set up so that you can't sue without first filing a complaint with an administrative agency. Sometimes you can't sue at all—the law is enforced solely by an administrative process.

Even more important, going to an administrative agency costs you no money, does not require a lawyer's help (though sometimes that's advisable), and keeps open the possibility of resolving the matter without a big fight. Almost all the labor and employment laws have procedures such as conciliation that are designed to reach an amicable settlement.

After filing a complaint with a government agency, an investigator is normally assigned to look into the case. Initially the investigator will talk to the complaining party, seeking to find out all the facts surrounding the complaint. Be sure to present any written documentation dealing with the case to the investigator—for example, in a discharge case the following types of documents might be available: letter of termination; previous written warning or disciplinary action; personnel evaluations; company manual; job description; and pay stubs. At this stage, you should also tell the investigator the names of other individuals who may have relevant information about the situation.

After obtaining information from you, the investigator will contact the company to hear its side of the story. The investigator will also contact third-party witnesses involved in the events.

When the investigation is completed, the agency will decide whether or not sufficient evidence exists to show that the law has been violated. If the agency decides that the complaint has merit, it will contact the employer and the employee and attempt to settle the case. If settlement is unsuccessful, the next step will depend on which law is involved and what agency is handling the case. For example, the NLRB will issue a complaint and hold a hearing. If the EEOC is involved, the next step would be to file a lawsuit in court.

If the agency decides that the law has not been violated, in some cases this is the end of the matter. For example, under the NLRA and the OSH Act it is solely up to the agency to decide whether or not to pursue a case. Under Title VII, however, even if the EEOC decides that the case has no merit, an individual can still file a lawsuit in court.

How long does the administrative process take? That depends on which agency is involved. For example, if the NLRB is involved, the investigation stage usually takes 30 to 45 days after a charge has been filed. The EEOC, however, generally takes several months and sometimes several years.

COURT PROCEDURES

What if, after going through the administrative process, you're still not satisfied? Many laws permit you to file suit in court after going through the process.

Or perhaps you haven't had to go through the administrative process. Some laws allow you to proceed directly to court and file a lawsuit.

But should you sue? That's a decision that is highly individual, but there are several factors to consider before making that decision. If you are suing your current employer, you should be aware that litigation causes hard feelings. Even though most of the employment laws have anti-retaliation provisions (see discussion in Chapter 4), your relationship with your employer can easily be adversely affected by litigation.

Second, you need to consider the likelihood that you will win your lawsuit. While no lawyer can predict with 100 percent accuracy the outcome of any lawsuit, a lawyer can give you a good indication of how likely it is that you can win. Litigation entails a tremendous amount of time and money, and such expenditures may make sense only where the prospects of winning are high.

Third, you should be aware that most lawsuits can take several years to reach a courtroom. In the meantime, parties to a lawsuit will be required to give testimony in **depositions** (answering questions during the pretrial discovery process), and lawyers will file legal motions dealing with certain aspects of the case. All of these procedures involve paying for the attorney's time and efforts as well as expending your own time participating in the process.

Litigation is, of course, a very valuable mechanism for vindicating your rights and receiving compensation for wrongdoing. However, satisfaction with the process is much higher among those who know what to expect before they decide to sue.

Defining the Terms Found in Federal Law

Most of the terms used in federal employment laws have an obvious meaning and don't need definition here. A few terms, however, bear special scrutiny.

Public Sector Employer. This term refers to employers that are governments, governmental agencies, or political subdivisions of a government. For example, a state department of motor vehicles, a city school district, and the United States Department of Agriculture are all public sector employers. The legal term for people who work for government employers is **public sector employees,** though in this book we refer to them simply as government employees.

Private Sector Employer. This term refers to nongovernmental employers. Any employer that is not a public sector employer is a private sector employer. Individuals who work for nongovernmental employers are called **private sector employees.**

Protected Class. The various antidiscrimination laws were passed to prohibit employers from taking adverse employment actions against individuals because of their membership in a protected class. Different laws define the protected class differently. For example, in **Title VII** the protected classes are race, sex, religion, national origin and color, whereas in the **ADA** the protected class is disability. Some state laws define the protected class as marital status or sexual orientation. The basis for all these laws is the premise that just because a person is in the protected class, he or she should be treated no differently than someone who is not a member of that class. It is a basis for ensuring equality of treatment, not preference in treatment.

Race. Title VII's prohibition against race discrimination does not protect only individuals who are members of minority racial groups, but individuals of all races. It includes not only African-Americans, Hispanics, Asians and Native Americans, but also Caucasians.

Religion. Title VII prohibits discrimination because of religion. Religion is not limited to membership in an established religious group, but includes the sincerely held religious beliefs of an individual whether or not he or she is connected to any institutional religious group. It also includes all aspects of religious observance, practice, and belief. For example, an individual who does not belong to any church, but sincerely believes she should read the Bible for two hours every day, would be covered by the law. If an employer fires her for reading the Bible during her lunch break, she is within the protection of Title VII forbidding religious discrimination.

Title VII grants an exemption to religious corporations and educational institutions. Such religiously affiliated employers can lawfully express a preference for employees of a particular religion. For example, a Catholic school can prefer to hire a teacher who is Catholic over one who is Protestant. This exemption applies only to religious preferences, however; it does not allow religious institutions to discriminate based on race, sex, national origin, age, or disability.

National Origin. Title VII prohibits discrimination based on national origin. National origin encompasses not only the place of origin of the individual and his or her ancestors, but also the possession by an individual of physical, cultural, or linguistic characteristics of a national origin group. For example, an employer hires individuals who are born in Mexico, but refuses to hire anyone who speaks with a Mexican accent; this employer has discriminated based on national origin. National origin does not include citizenship status, however. Thus, under Title VII the employer can have a policy of requiring all employees to be U.S. citizens without discriminating based on national origin. (Such a policy, however, would run afoul of the requirements of the **Immigration Reform and Control Act [IRCA]**, which prohibits discrimination based on citizenship status.)

Citizenship. IRCA prohibits discrimination based on citizens tus. As that term is defined in the statute, citizenship status in only those individuals who are actually U.S. citizens or lawfully admitted aliens who have applied for naturalization. Thus, a lawfully admitted alien who has resided in the United States for ten years and has taken no steps to apply for citizenship can lawfully be discriminated against because he is not a citizen. However, a lawfully admitted alien who has taken steps to become naturalized cannot be denied a job just because he is not currently a citizen.

Sex. Title VII prohibits discrimination based on sex. Sex means a person's gender, not his or her sexual orientation. It has also been defined to include pregnancy, childbirth and related medical conditions. Thus, an employer firing a woman because she became pregnant has discriminated against her based on her sex; but an employer that refuses to promote a woman because she is a lesbian has not violated Title VII (however, that employer may be in violation of state or city/municipal law in those jurisdictions that prohibit sexual orientation discrimination).

Disability. Both the **ADA** and the **Rehabilitation Act** prohibit discrimination against qualified individuals with a disability. An individual with a disability is one who:

1. has a physical or mental impairment that substantially limits a major life activity;
2. has a record of having such a physical or mental impairment; or
3. is regarded as having such an impairment.

The term is defined broadly to include any physiologically based impairment or any mental or psychological impairment. It does not, however, include mere physical characteristics or cultural, economic or environmental impairments. For example, an individual with dyslexia has a disability, but an individual who is illiterate does not. A person who is a dwarf has a disability but a person who is short does not.

To fall within the statute, the impairment must cause a substantial limitation to a major life activity. A temporary condition, such as a broken leg or a cold, would not be considered a substantial limitation. Major life activities include walking, eating, seeing, speaking, and working.

The second meaning of the term includes persons who no longer have a disability but have a record of a disability, such as a person who successfully recovered from tuberculosis, or a person who was diagnosed as having cancer but in fact did not have, or no longer has, cancer.

The third meaning of the term includes individuals who have a condition that does not substantially limit their activity, but the employer believes they are so limited. An example would be a worker who has high blood pressure and is denied a promotion because the employer believes that the stress of the job would cause a heart attack.

In order to be protected under these statutes, the individual not only has to have a disability, but must also be **qualified.** People with a disability are qualified if they "satisfy the requisite skill, experience, education and other job-related requirements." For example, a person with epilepsy applies for a job as a teacher but does not possess a teaching certificate; he or she is not a "qualified" individual and therefore is not protected under the law, despite the disability.

Certain types of conditions are not considered disabilities under the ADA. Disability does not include: homosexuality, transvestism, transsexualism, bisexuality, sexual behavior disorders, compulsive gambling, kleptomania, pyromania, or current illegal drug use.

Employees Engaged in Interstate Commerce. The **Fair Labor Standards Act (FLSA)** applies to employees engaged in **interstate commerce.** The Wage and Hour Division of the Department of Labor has identified five general categories of employees who are considered to be engaged in interstate commerce:

1. employees participating in the actual movement of commerce: for example, employees in the telephone, transportation or insurance industries;
2. employees performing work related to the **instrumentalities of com-**

merce: for example, employees who maintain and repair roads and bridges, and employees who work at airports and bus stations.

3. employees who regularly cross state lines in performing their duties, such as traveling salespersons;

4. employees who produce or work on goods for commerce: for example, assembly workers in auto plants, coal miners, and shipping department employees; and

5. employees who work in a closely related process or occupation essential to producing goods for commerce: for example, employees who build machines used in auto plants.

■

Labor and Employment Laws

This appendix provides a handy summary of the laws discussed in this book. It contains a general description of which types of employers are regulated by each law, what each law requires, and how the law is enforced. See appropriate sections of the main text for more on each law.

EMPLOYMENT DISCRIMINATION LAWS

These federal laws generally prohibit employers from discriminating against employees and applicants. They cover hiring, firing and terms and conditions of employment. They protect employees/applicants who are members of an identified class of protected individuals.

Title VII of the Civil Rights Act of 1964 (Title VII)

This is perhaps the most important federal antidiscrimination law.

What It Does: Prohibits employment discrimination based on race, color, religion, sex and national origin.

Who Is Covered: All government and private sector employers employing at least 15 employees. Unions having at least 15 members and employment agencies are also covered.

Where to Find It in the Law Books: 42 U.S. Code, secs. 2000e–2000e-17.

Where to Find More Information: Equal Employment Opportunity Commission, 1801 L Street, N.W., Washington, DC 20507. There are regional offices of the EEOC in many major cities throughout the United States. The EEOC has brochures that explain the law and describe the charge-filing process. You can obtain these brochures by calling (202) 663-4900.

There are also several private organizations that deal with problems relating to employment discrimination—NAACP Legal Defense and Education Fund, 99 Hudson Street, 16th Floor, New York, NY 10013; National Organization for Women Legal Defense and Education Fund, 99 Hudson Street, New York, NY 10013; National Women's Law Center, 1616 P Street, N.W., Suite 100, Washington, DC 20036; Mexican American Legal Defense and Education Fund, 634 South Spring Street, 11th Floor, Los Angeles, CA 90014; Asian-American Legal Defense and Education Fund, 99 Hudson Street, 12th Floor, New York, NY 10013; National Organization for Women, 1000 16th Street, N.W., Suite 700, Washington, DC 20036; 9to5, National Association of Working Women, 614 Superior Avenue, N.W., Suite 852, Cleveland, OH 44113.

Who Enforces It: The Equal Employment Opportunity Commission (**EEOC**) investigates complaints of Title VII violations. It also has the authority to file lawsuits in federal court to enforce the statute. Indi-

---

FINDING FEDERAL LAWS

Federal laws are collected in a series of books called the U.S. Code. Every federal law is assigned a title number and a section number. The title number is the general category for grouping laws dealing with related matters. For example, many labor laws are found in Title 29. The section number refers to the specific place within the title where a law can be found. Thus, you can find the ADEA in Title 29 of the U.S. Code beginning at section 621. This is written as "29 U.S. Code, sec. 621."

viduals may also file lawsuits in either state or federal court alleging that their rights under the law have been violated.

Going to the EEOC: First, you are required to file a charge with the EEOC. You must file the charge in writing and describe the conduct (by an employer, union or employment agency) that you claim violates the law. You can file in one of the EEOC regional offices, which exist in most major cities. The courts will dismiss any lawsuit that is filed without first filing a charge with the EEOC and giving it a chance to investigate the claim.

Second, there are time limits for filing a charge with the EEOC. If you miss the deadline for filing a charge, you lose your opportunity to have your case heard either before the EEOC or in court. The time limit for filing depends on whether what you're complaining about is against the antidiscrimination law in your state.

In states that have an antidiscrimination law covering the matter, you must first file a charge with the state agency responsible for enforcing that law before you can file with the EEOC. The state agency must have at least 60 days to investigate the complaint. After 60 days, you can then file the charge with the EEOC. The deadline for filing the charge with the EEOC is 300 days from the date the unlawful discrimination occurred, or within 30 days after the state agency finishes its proceedings, whichever happens first.

In states that do not cover the matter in an antidiscrimination law, you must file the charge with the EEOC within 180 days from the date of the discriminatory act.

After your charge is filed with the EEOC, the agency investigates the complaint to determine whether there is reasonable cause to believe the law was violated. If the EEOC decides there is reasonable cause, it enters into **conciliation** with your employer and tries to settle the case. If settlement is unsuccessful, the EEOC will send you a letter informing you that you have 90 days to file a lawsuit in court. This is called a **right to sue** letter.

Although the EEOC has the authority to file lawsuits in court, it does so only in a small percentage of cases. Most of the time, you must pursue a lawsuit on your own.

If, after the investigation, the EEOC decides there is no reasonable cause to believe the law was violated, it will still send you a right to sue letter. The law gives you the right to have a court determine the merits of the complaint, even when the EEOC decides there is no merit. The statute of limitations for filing the lawsuit is 90 days from the date of receiving the right to sue letter. (**Statutes of limitation** are time deadlines set by law for filing a lawsuit. If a suit is filed after the time limit set by the statute, it will almost always be dismissed by the court.)

If You're a Federal Employee. If you're an employee of the federal government, you use a different procedure. All federal government agencies have EEO counselors whose job is to try to resolve discrimination complaints. Thus, the federal employee must first file any charge with the EEO counselor within 45 days of the date of the discriminatory act. The counselor investigates the matter and attempts to resolve the complaint. If you're not satisfied with the counselor's proposed settlement, you must, within 15 days, either request a hearing on the complaint or request a decision by the head of the agency without a hearing. If you request a hearing, it is conducted by an independent administrative law judge, who issues a decision. The judge's decision is sent to the agency head, who may reject, accept or modify it.

After the agency head issues a decision, you have three options: accept the decision of the agency head, file an appeal with the EEOC within 30 days, or file a lawsuit in court within 90 days.

If you decide to appeal to the EEOC, the EEOC has 180 days to review the file and make a final decision. If you are not satisfied with the EEOC's final decision, you can file a lawsuit in court within 90 days of receiving the EEOC decision.

If You Win: What will you get if you win? The remedies available include both **injunctive relief** and a **make-whole remedy.** In cases involving intentional discrimination (but not adverse impact), a court will also award **compensatory damages** and, where appropriate, **punitive damages.** (See box on page 158 for a discussion of all these terms.)

Compensatory and punitive damage amounts are capped based on the size of the employer. For example, small employers with fewer than 101 employees are liable for no more than $50,000 total in compensatory and punitive damages; employers with more than 500 employees are liable for no more than $300,000 total. In adverse impact cases, only make-whole and injunctive relief are available. The court in its discretion may (in either type of case) award attorney's fees to the prevailing party.

Section 1981

This is a very old law, dating from the years just after the Civil War.

What It Does: Prohibits employment discrimination based on race or ethnicity.

Who Is Covered: All government and private sector employers, regardless of size.

Where to Find It in the Law Books: 42 U.S. Code, sec. 1981.

Who Enforces It: Private individuals, through lawsuits. There is no

---

REMEDYING YOUR LOSS

Compensatory Damages. This has two different meanings, depending on whether the lawsuit is based on a labor statute or on state common law. **Statutory compensatory damages** are compensation for the *indirect* injuries you suffer as a natural consequence of the wrongdoer's act. An example is payment for pain and suffering and medical expenses you incur as a result of the law's violation. Compensation for your *direct* injuries are termed **make-whole remedies** in labor statutes (see the definition on the next page). **Common-law compensatory damages** include compensation not only for your indirect injuries, but also for direct injuries that are the usual result of the wrong-doing, such as back pay owed if you were wrongfully terminated.

Injunctive Relief. This is a court order directed at wrongdoers, requiring them to engage in certain types of action. The order might tell them to stop violating the law and not do it again in the future. Or an order might require them to take certain affirmative steps to restore things to the position they would have been in had the law not been violated, such as hiring you if you were wrongfully denied a job.

---

federal agency with authority to enforce this law. Individuals may file lawsuits in either state or federal court alleging violations of their rights under this statute.

Going to Court: You can file suit directly in court for violations. You don't have to take any administrative steps. The time limit for filing the lawsuit is based on the state statute of limitations for personal injury suits—usually two or three years from the date of the event giving rise to the suit.

If You Win: You might get injunctive relief, make-whole remedies, compensatory and punitive damages, and reasonable attorney's fees.

Section 1983

This law is a companion to Section 1981, and also dates from the years after the Civil War.

Make-Whole Remedy. This remedy puts you into the position you would have been in had there been no violation of the law. For example, let's say you're illegally terminated from a job. The make-whole remedy would include: reinstatement to the job; payment of the wages you would have earned (with interest) had you remained employed; payment of any bonuses, vacation pay, or other types of payments you would have earned had you remained employed; accrual of seniority and pension benefits you would have been credited with had you remained employed; and payment for any medical expenses you incurred that would have been covered under the employer's health insurance plan. The elements of the make-whole remedy will vary depending on the type of injury suffered.

Punitive Damages. These damages are intended to punish the wrongdoer *and* deter others from engaging in similar conduct. The money goes to you, not the government. Courts award these damages when the wrongdoer acts with malice or reckless indifference to your rights. Only in very limited circumstances are punitive damages available in labor and employment law cases.

What It Does: Prohibits discrimination in employment because of membership in a protected class and limits the ability of an employer to interfere with the constitutional rights of its employees.

Who Is Covered: All state and local government employers regardless of size.

Where to Find It in the Law Books: 42 U.S. Code, sec. 1983.

Who Enforces It: Private individuals, through lawsuits. There is no government agency with authority to enforce this law. Individuals may file lawsuits in either state or federal court alleging violations of their rights under this statute.

Going to Court: You can file suit directly in court for violations. You don't have to take any administrative steps. The time limit for filing the lawsuit is based on the state statute of limitations for personal injury suits—usually two or three years from the date of the event giving rise to the suit.

If You Win: You might get injunctive relief, make-whole remedies, compensatory damages and reasonable attorney's fees. Punitive damages may be awarded against individuals (not the government entity) when they act with reckless disregard of a plaintiff's rights.

The Age Discrimination in Employment Act (ADEA)

What It Does: Prohibits employment discrimination based on the fact that the employee or applicant is 40 years or older.

Who Is Covered: Public and private sector employers employing at least 20 people, as well as unions and employment agencies.

Where to Find It in the Law Books: 29 U.S. Code, secs. 621–634.

Where to Find More Information: The EEOC and the American Association of Retired Persons, 1909 K Street, N.W., Washington, DC 20049.

Who Enforces It: The EEOC has enforcement authority under the ADEA both to investigate complaints and to file lawsuits. Individuals may also file lawsuits in either state or federal court alleging violations of the ADEA.

Going to the EEOC: Procedures are slightly different than those for enforcing Title VII. As with Title VII, you must file a written charge with the EEOC. The time limits for filing this charge depend on whether there is a state law that prohibits age discrimination. The same 180-day/300-day time limits apply as discussed under Title VII. The one difference is that in those states with age discrimination laws, you are not required to file with the state agency before filing with the EEOC. As long as you file with both, the order of filing doesn't matter. The remainder of the enforcement procedure is the same: an investigation, an attempt to conciliate and the issuance of a right to sue letter.

The procedures for federal employees are the same as those under Title VII.

Going to Court: You can't file suit without first going to the EEOC and getting a right to sue letter. You have 90 days from the date you receive the right to sue letter to file a lawsuit in court.

If You Win: The remedies available under the ADEA include injunctive relief and a make-whole remedy. In those cases where the employer acted with reckless disregard for the rights of the employee, the employer must pay the employee **liquidated damages.** For example, if the employer owes the employee $25,000 in back pay, liquidated damages would equal an additional $25,000. The courts also award attorney's fees to successful plaintiffs.

Title I of the Americans with Disabilities Act (ADA)

What It Does: Prohibits employment discrimination against qualified individuals with a disability.

Who Is Covered: All state and local government employers and private sector employers employing at least 15 employees. Unions having at least 15 members and employment agencies are also covered.

Where to Find It in the Law Books: 42 U.S. Code, secs. 12101–12111.

Where to Find More Information: The EEOC. Several private organizations also focus on disability rights issues—The Disability Rights Education and Defense Fund, Inc., 2212 6th Street, Berkeley, CA 94710; Mental Health Law Project, 1101 15th Street, N.W., Suite 1212, Washington, DC 20005; Disability Rights Center, 2500 Q Street, N.W., Suite 121, Washington, DC 20007.

Who Enforces It: The EEOC has the authority to investigate complaints and file lawsuits under the ADA. Individuals may also file lawsuits in either state or federal court alleging violations of the ADA after exhausting the administrative procedures.

Going to the EEOC: The administrative procedures under the ADA are exactly the same as those required under Title VII.

If You Win: The exact same remedies available under Title VII are awarded under the ADA.

The Rehabilitation Act

What It Does: Prohibits employment discrimination against qualified individuals with disabilities.

Who Is Covered: Executive branch agencies of the federal government, the U.S. Postal Service, federal government contractors and subcontractors whose contracts are in excess of $2,500, and programs that receive federal funds.

Where to Find It in the Law Books: 29 U.S. Code, secs. 706(8), 791, 793–794(a).

Where to Find More Information: The same private organizations that are concerned with legal issues under the ADA are also familiar with issues arising under the Rehabilitation Act.

Who Enforces It: The enforcement mechanisms for this statute vary depending on who the employer is. If the employer is the federal government or the U.S. Postal Service, then the EEOC has the authority to investigate complaints and file lawsuits. If the employer is a federal contractor or subcontractor, the responsibility for enforcement lies with the Office of Federal Contract Compliance (**OFCCP**) of the Department of Labor. The OFCCP has offices located in ten cities across the United States: Boston, New York, Philadelphia, Atlanta, Chicago, Dallas, Kansas City (Missouri), Denver, San Francisco and Seattle. If the employer is a program that receives federal funding, private individuals can file a lawsuit directly; there is no government agency responsible for enforcement under these circumstances.

How to Enforce the Rehabilitation Act Against the Federal Government: The enforcement process is exactly the same as the process used by federal government employees under Title VII. The remedies available are also the same as under Title VII.

How to Enforce the Rehabilitation Act Against Federal Contractors: An individual must file a written complaint with the OFCCP within 180 days of the date of the unlawful discrimination. The OFCCP investigates and determines what type of action to take.

If the OFCCP decides that the law has been violated, it enters into conciliation with the employer and tries to settle the case. If settlement is unsuccessful, a hearing is held before an ALJ. The decision of the ALJ is appealable to the Department of Labor. The final decision of the Department of Labor can be appealed to the federal district court.

If a violation is found, the government may terminate the contract, debar the contractor from further government business, or order the contractor to make whole the employee who was discriminated against.

Individuals cannot file their own lawsuits alleging violations of the Rehabilitation Act. The OFCCP has the exclusive authority to enforce the law.

How to Enforce the Rehabilitation Act Against Programs That Receive Federal Funds: There is no government agency that enforces the Rehabilitation Act against recipients of federal funds. Individuals may file a lawsuit directly in federal court. There is no uniform statute of limitations for filing a lawsuit. The deadline is based on the most closely analogous state statute of limitations, which can vary from one year in some states to six years in others. Successful plaintiffs are entitled to injunctive relief, make-whole remedies, compensatory and punitive damages and reasonable attorney's fees.

Uniformed Services Employment and Reemployment Rights Act of 1994 (USSERA)

What It Does: Prohibits employment discrimination because of an employee's or applicant's past, current, or future military obligations. It also requires employers to reinstate to their former jobs, upon honorable completion of their military duty, employees who have served in the uniformed services.

Who Is Covered: All public and private sector employers regardless of size.

Where to Find It in the Law Books: 38 U.S. Code, secs. 4301–4333.

Where to Find More Information: Department of Labor, Veterans' Employment and Training Service, 200 Constitution Avenue, N.W., Washington, DC 20210; Veterans of Foreign Wars, 406 W. 34th Street, Kansas City, MO 64111; National Veterans Legal Services Project, 2001 S Street, N.W., Suite 702, Washington, DC 20009.

Who Enforces It: The Office of Veterans' Employment and Training Service (**VETS**) of the Department of Labor has the responsibility for investigating complaints under the USERRA. Individuals may also file lawsuits in court to enforce their rights.

Going to VETS: An individual who is employed by a state or local government or a private sector employer is not required to first file a complaint with VETS. He or she may file a lawsuit directly in court, without following any administrative procedure. There is no statute of limitations for filing a lawsuit. The only rule is that a plaintiff may not unreasonably delay filing a suit so as to cause prejudice to the defendant's ability to present its case.

An individual may, however, file a charge with the VETS office. Filing an administrative charge may help to resolve the problem without the necessity of a lawsuit.

Once a charge is filed, VETS is required to investigate and, if it finds merit, attempt to resolve the problem. VETS notifies the charging party of the outcome of the investigation and provides information about further enforcement options.

If VETS is unsuccessful in resolving the charge, the individual can ask the Department of Labor to refer the case to the U.S. attorney general for prosecution. It is within the discretion of the attorney general to decide whether to prosecute the case. The individual always has the option of bringing his or her own private lawsuit in court.

An individual who is employed by the federal government cannot file a lawsuit directly in court. Federal employees must first file a charge with the VETS office. If, after finding merit to the charge, VETS is unsuccessful in its attempt to settle the case, the employee may request that the charge be referred to the Office of Special Counsel for the Merit Systems Protection Board (**MSPB**). It is within the discretion of the special counsel to decide whether to prosecute the case before the MSPB. If the special counsel decides not to prosecute, the individual may then file a complaint directly with the MSPB.

If You Win: The remedies available include injunctive relief, make-whole remedies and liquidated damages. The court may, in its discretion, award reasonable attorney's fees.

Immigration Reform and Control Act (IRCA)

What It Does: Prohibits discrimination with regard to hiring, recruiting, or discharging employees based on national origin or citizenship status. It also prohibits employers from hiring illegal aliens and requires employers to verify the work eligibility status of all applicants for employment.

Who Is Covered: All private sector employers that employ three or more employees.

Where to Find It in the Law Books: 8 U.S. Code, secs. 1324a–1324c.

Where to Find More Information: Department of Justice, Office of the Special Counsel for Immigration-Related Unfair Employment Practices, P.O. Box 27728, Washington, DC 20038, (800) 255-7688; League of United Latin American Citizens, 900 East Karen, Suite C215, Las Vegas, NV 89109; Mexican American Legal Defense and Educational Fund, 634 South Spring Street, 11th Floor, Los Angeles, CA 90014.

Who Enforces It: The Office of the Special Counsel for Immigration-Related Unfair Employment Practices (Special Counsel), Department of Justice, has the authority to investigate and prosecute charges. Individuals cannot file private lawsuits; they must use the administrative process.

Going to the Special Counsel: An individual who believes his or her rights under IRCA were violated must file a written complaint with the special counsel within 180 days from the date of the alleged violation. The special counsel investigates the case and within 120 days decides whether or not to prosecute the case. If the special counsel decides to prosecute the case, he or she files a complaint before a Department of Justice ALJ. If the special counsel decides not to prosecute the case, the counsel must notify the charging party, who then has 90 days to file his or her own complaint before the Department of Justice ALJ.

The ALJ holds a hearing and issues a decision. The decision of the ALJ can be appealed to the federal court of appeals within 60 days after the decision is issued.

If You Win: The remedy for a violation is a make-whole order. An employer may also be subject to civil fines of between $250 and $3,000. (**Civil fines** are paid to the government, not to the plaintiff.)

Executive Orders

Executive orders are issued by the President. They regulate employers who do business with federal government agencies.

Executive Order 12,086—What It Does: Prohibits employment discrimination based on race, color, religion, sex, and national origin.

Executive Order 11,141—What It Does: Prohibits employment discrimination based on age.

Executive Order 12,989—What It Does: Prohibits executive branch agencies from entering into contracts with any employer that knowingly hires illegal aliens.

Who Is Covered by Executive Orders: All private sector employers that have contracts with the federal government.

Where to Find Executive Orders in the Law Books: Executive orders are reprinted in Title 3 of the Code of Federal Regulations.

Who Enforces Executive Orders: The Office of Federal Contract Compliance (**OFCCP**) of the Department of Labor is responsible for ensuring compliance with the antidiscrimination mandates of Executive Orders 12,086 and 11,141. The OFCCP has offices located in ten cities across the United States: Boston, New York, Philadelphia, Atlanta, Chicago, Dallas, Kansas City (Missouri), Denver, San Francisco, and Seattle. Each federal agency is responsible for ensuring contractor compliance under Executive Order 12,989. Individuals cannot file lawsuits in court to enforce executive orders; they may, however, file complaints with the appropriate agency notifying it of possible noncompliance with the executive order.

Enforcement Procedures for Executive Orders: If the agency responsible for ensuring compliance with an executive order determines, after an investigation, that the contractor is not in compliance, it will notify the contractor of its decision. The contractor has the opportunity to contest the decision, in which case a hearing is held before an ALJ. The decision of the ALJ is appealable to the Department of Labor. The final decision of the Department of Labor can be appealed to a federal district court.

What the Consequences of Noncompliance with an Executive Order Are: A contractor found to be in noncompliance may have its current contract terminated, may be debarred from entering into future government contracts, or may be required to take appropriate action to bring it into compliance with the mandates of the Executive Order.

UNION-MANAGEMENT LAWS

These laws prohibit discrimination in employment because an employee has joined, or refused to join, a labor organization, or because an employee has engaged, or refused to engage, in union activity. The laws also impose restrictions on labor organizations and establish election procedures for determining when employees have chosen to be represented by a union.

National Labor Relations Act (NLRA)

What It Does: Regulates the labor-management relationship and prohibits discrimination based on union activity.

Who Is Covered: All private sector employers that have an impact on interstate commerce. The dollar volume of business generated by a company determines whether its operations impact interstate commerce. For example, the NLRA covers retail and service establishments with annual gross receipts of at least $500,000. Labor unions are also covered.

Specifically excluded from coverage are public sector employers, railway and airline employers, supervisory and managerial employees and individuals who are employed as agricultural laborers.

Where to Find It in the Law Books: 29 U.S. Code, secs. 141–197.

Where to Find More Information: National Labor Relations Board, 1099 14th Street, N.W., Washington, DC 20570. The NLRB has free pamphlets that explain the rights and procedures of the law, available by calling (202) 273-1991. Local labor unions in your community may also have information concerning employee rights under this law.

Who Enforces It: The National Labor Relations Board (**NLRB**) has the exclusive authority to investigate charges and prosecute complaints. With few exceptions, individuals cannot file their own lawsuit in court.

Going to the NLRB: Individuals who believe their rights have been violated must file a written charge with the NLRB within six months of the date of the alleged violation. There are regional offices located in most major cities. The NLRB investigates the case and decides if there is reasonable cause to believe the law was violated. If it decides that there is no reasonable cause, it will dismiss the charge and so inform the charging party by letter. The charging party has the right to appeal the dismissal to the Office of the General Counsel of the NLRB in Washington, D.C. The decision of the general counsel is final and nonappealable.

If the NLRB decides that there is reasonable cause to believe the law was violated, it will first attempt to settle the case. If settlement is unsuccessful, a hearing will be held before an ALJ. The decision of the ALJ is appealed to the board of the NLRB. The board's decision is subject to review by the federal court of appeals.

The exception to the general rule that an individual cannot file a private lawsuit occurs when a union violates its duty of fair representation. In that case an employee may file his or her own lawsuit in either federal or state court. The time limit for filing such a lawsuit is six months. Employers also have the right to file a lawsuit in federal court to recover damages for losses sustained as a result of a union engaging in a secondary boycott. There is no uniform time limit for such a lawsuit—it varies based on the jurisdiction in which the suit is filed. Some deadlines are as short as one year or as long as three years.

If You Win: The remedies for violations are injunctive relief, make-whole remedies, and a requirement that the offending party post a notice in the workplace, or at the union's place of business, informing the employees of the outcome of the case. The remedies in cases alleging a violation of the union's duty of fair representation are make-whole orders and compensatory damages; in appropriate cases a court may award reasonable attorney's fees.

Railway Labor Act (RLA)

What It Does: Regulates the labor-management relationship and prohibits discrimination based on union activity.

Who Is Covered: All railroads and airlines.

Where to Find It in the Law Books: 45 U.S. Code, secs. 151–188.

Where to Find More Information: Chief of Staff, National Mediation Board, Suite 250 East, 1301 K Street, N.W., Washington, DC 20572.

Who Enforces It: There are two federal administrative agencies responsible for enforcing the RLA. The National Mediation Board (**NMB**) regulates the union election process and acts as mediator in helping employers and unions negotiate contracts. The National Railroad Adjustment Board (**NRAB**) acts as an arbitration agency to resolve disputes concerning the application and interpretation of contracts between unions and employers. The offices of the NRAB are in Chicago, Illinois. Only if a dispute does not fall within the jurisdiction of either the NMB or the NRAB may an individual file his or her own lawsuit in federal court.

Going to Court: In those cases dealing with employer discrimination where there is no union representation, or cases alleging a violation of the duty of fair representation, individuals can file private lawsuits in federal court. The time limit for filing a lawsuit is six months from the date of the alleged violation. Once a union represents the employees, however, almost all disputes must be submitted to an Adjustment Board.

If You Win: Injunctive relief and make-whole remedies are awarded to the successful plaintiff. The courts are divided on whether punitive damages are available. In some cases, criminal penalties can be imposed on employers, but this sanction is rarely used.

Federal Labor Relations Act (FLRA)

What It Does: Regulates the labor-management relationship and prohibits discrimination based on union activity.

Who Is Covered: Federal government executive agency employers. Supervisory and managerial personnel are excluded from the protections of the law.

Where to Find It in the Law Books: 5 U.S. Code, secs. 7101–7135.

Where to Find More Information: Federal Labor Relations Authority, 607 14th Street, N.W., Washington, DC 20424.

Who Enforces It: There are two federal agencies with authority under the FLRA. The Federal Labor Relations Authority (**FLR Authority**) has the exclusive responsibility to investigate and adjudicate complaints alleging violations of rights under the FLRA and to regulate the election process. The **Federal Service Impasses Panel** provides assistance to unions and employers in resolving impasses that occur during contract negotiations. This agency does not handle problems or complaints filed by individual employees. Individuals may not file private lawsuits under this statute; they must file their complaints with the FLR Authority.

Going to the FLR Authority: The procedures for enforcing the law are modeled after those found in the NRLA. An aggrieved employee must file a charge with the regional office of the authority within six months of the discriminatory act. The authority investigates the charge, and if reasonable cause exists to believe the FLRA was violated and attempts to settle are unsuccessful, a hearing will be held before an ALJ. The ALJ decision is appealable to the three members who compose the adjudicatory board of the authority. The decisions of this panel are appealable to the federal court of appeals.

If You Win: Remedies for violations of the FLRA are injunctive relief, make-whole remedies, and a notice posted at the workplace informing employees of the outcome of the case.

Labor-Management Reporting and Disclosure Act (LMRDA)

What It Does: Regulates the operation of labor organizations, their relationship to their members and the conduct of internal union elections.

Who Is Covered: All private sector labor unions.

Where to Find It in the Law Books: 29 U.S. Code, secs. 401–531.

Where to Find More Information: Public Affairs Team, Office of the American Workplace, Department of Labor, Room N5402, 200 Constitution Avenue, N.W., Washington, DC 20210. This office has free publications describing rights and responsibilities under the LMRDA that can be obtained by calling (202) 219-6098.

Who Enforces It: Individual union members possess a private right to bring a lawsuit in federal court to enforce most of the provisions of the LMRDA. The time limit for filing most individual lawsuits under the LMRDA is based on the most closely analogous state statute of limitations; there is no uniform time limit.

There is an exception, however, with regard to challenges to internal union elections. In such cases, a union member must first invoke and attempt to exhaust any internal union procedures available under the union constitution and bylaws for challenging elections. If the union member is dissatisfied with the outcome of the internal union process, he or she may then file a complaint with the Office of Labor-Management Standards (**LMS**), Department of Labor, within one month after the internal union procedures have been completed or within three months after the member first invoked such procedures. LMS has district offices located in major cities throughout the United States.

The Office of LMS investigates the complaint, and if it determines reasonable cause exists to believe the law was violated and that the violation may have affected the outcome of the election, it will attempt to settle the case. If settlement is unsuccessful, the secretary of labor will file suit in court. The remedy for a successful challenge to a union election is to void the results of the election and direct the holding of a new election.

If You Win: An individual who brings a private cause of action under the LMRDA is entitled to injunctive relief, compensatory damages, make-whole relief where appropriate, and in limited circumstances reasonable attorney's fees.

WAGE AND HOUR LAWS

These laws set minimum wage amounts that employers must pay to certain classes of employees, and limit the hours of work for certain employees.

Fair Labor Standards Act (FLSA)

What It Does: Sets minimum wage and overtime requirements and regulates the employment of child labor.

Who Is Covered: Private sector employers who have at least two employees engaged in interstate commerce activities or in the production of goods for interstate commerce and whose annual volume of business is at least $500,000. Public sector employers, hospitals and educational institutions are also covered.

Also, individual employees who are engaged in interstate commerce activities are covered even if their employer does not gross $500,000 a year.

Where to Find It in the Law Books: 29 U.S. Code, secs. 201–219.

Where to Find More Information: Department of Labor, Wage and Hour Division, 200 Constitution Avenue, N.W., Washington, DC 20210. Free pamphlets explaining the law are available by calling (202) 219-7316.

Who Enforces It: The Wage and Hour Division of the Department of Labor has the authority to investigate complaints and file lawsuits in court. Any individual may also institute legal action in state or federal court. There is no requirement that an individual file an administrative charge before going to court. An individual may, however, file a charge with the Wage and Hour Division.

Going to the Wage and Hour Division: Once an individual files a charge, the division will investigate, and if it finds a violation, attempt to get the employer to voluntarily agree to a settlement. If settlement is not possible, the Department of Labor may file a lawsuit; it is not, however, required to file suit.

Going to Court: The statute of limitations for filing a lawsuit is two years, or if the employer acted with reckless disregard as to whether its conduct violated the law, the deadline is extended to three years. An individual can file a lawsuit in either state or federal court.

If You Win: Injunctive relief, payment of the wages owed, liquidated damages in an amount equal to the wages owed, and reasonable attorney's fees are awarded. An employer can avoid having to pay liquidated damages if it can prove that it acted in good faith and with reasonable grounds for believing its actions were legal.

Equal Pay Act (EPA)

What It Does: Requires employers to pay equal wages to male and female employees who are performing substantially equivalent work.

Who Is Covered: The same employers that are covered under the FLSA.

Where to Find It in the Law Books: 29 U.S. Code, sec. 206(d).

Where to Find More Information: The EEOC; 9to5, National Association of Working Women, 614 Superior Avenue, N.W., Suite 852, Cleveland, OH 44113; National Organization for Women, 1000 16th Street, N.W., Suite 700, Washington, DC 20036.

Who Enforces It: The EEOC has the authority to investigate complaints and file lawsuits. Individual workers may also file lawsuits.

Going to the EEOC: Individuals are not required to file a charge with the EEOC before filing a lawsuit. If a charge is filed, however, the EEOC will investigate and determine whether there is reasonable cause to believe a violation has occurred. If they find a violation, they will attempt conciliation. If settlement is unsuccessful, they may file a lawsuit but are not required to do so.

Going to Court: Individuals may file a private lawsuit in either state or federal court. The time limit is two years, or if the employer acted with reckless disregard as to whether its conduct violated the law, the deadline is extended to three years.

If You Win: The remedies are the same as those available under the FLSA.

Walsh-Healey Public Contracts Act

What It Does: Regulates wage payments.

Who Is Covered: Federal government contractors where the contract is for the purchase of supplies in excess of $10,000.

Where to Find It in the Law Books: 41 U.S. Code, secs. 35–45.

Who Enforces It: The Wage and Hour Division, Department of Labor. Only in very limited circumstances can employees file a lawsuit in court.

Going to the Department of Labor: Employees can notify the agency with which the employer has its contract of the employer's noncompliance, and that agency will notify the Department of Labor. If the secretary of labor determines that the contractor has violated the wage requirements, it can withhold payment under the contract and use the money to pay the required wage amounts to the employees. It can also debar the contractor from further government work.

Davis-Bacon Act

What It Does: Requires employers to pay construction workers the prevailing area wage and fringe benefit rate.

Who Is Covered: Employers with federal construction project contracts whose contract value exceeds $2,000.

Where to Find It in the Law Books: 40 U.S. Code, secs. 276a–276a-7.

Who Enforces It: This law is enforced by the Wage and Hour Division, Department of Labor. The same process used for enforcing the Walsh-Healey Act applies to Davis-Bacon.

Service Contract Act

What It Does: Regulates the wage payments to employees working under federal service contracts.

Who Is Covered: Federal contractors and subcontractors who provide services to the federal government.

Where to Find It in the Law Books: 41 U.S. Code, secs. 351–358.

Who Enforces It: The Wage and Hour Division, Department of

Labor. The enforcement process is the same as that for Walsh-Healey and Davis-Bacon.

WORKPLACE SAFETY LAWS

These laws have established federal agencies with the authority to promulgate health and safety rules for the workplace, and require employers to comply with such standards.

Occupational Safety and Health Act (OSH Act)

What It Does: Regulates workplace safety and health.

Who Is Covered: Private sector employers affecting interstate commerce, but excluding the mining industry.

Where to Find It in the Law Books: 29 U.S. Code, secs. 651–678.

Where to Find More Information: Occupational Safety and Health Administration, 200 Constitution Avenue, N.W., Washington, DC 20210. A catalog of publications dealing with health and safety issues is available by calling (202) 219-4667.

Who Enforces It: The Occupational Safety and Health Administration (**OSHA**) has the exclusive authority for enforcing the OSH Act. Individual workers cannot file their own lawsuits.

Going to OSHA: Employees can file either oral or written complaints with OSHA alleging that a workplace condition constitutes a safety or health hazard. There are regional and area offices located in cities throughout the United States. Upon receiving a complaint, OSHA will decide if there are reasonable grounds for believing a violation of the law exists. If it has reason to believe there is a violation, either it will send a letter to the employer regarding the alleged violation and suggesting how to correct the problem, or it will send an inspector to the workplace to conduct an on-site safety inspection. OSHA also has the authority to conduct workplace inspections at its own discretion.

During an inspection, the OSHA investigator will meet with the employer, explain the nature of the inspection, and review employer documents pertaining to workplace injuries and hazards. The inspector will then "walk around" the plant and physically inspect the workplace. The employer and a representative of the employees are allowed to accompany the inspector on the walk-around. The inspector will also talk with employees and ask them questions. At the end of the inspection, the inspector will informally tell the employer of any possible violations that may have been uncovered during the investigation.

If violations are uncovered, OSHA will send the employer a citation that lists each violation and describes what the employer must do to fix the problem. The employer may also be fined a monetary penalty, the amount of which is determined by the seriousness of the violation. An employer can also be subject to criminal liability and imprisonment for willful violation of an OSHA standard that results in an employee's death. The citation is required to be posted at the workplace in the areas where the violations exist. If the employer contests the citation or the penalty, it must file a notice within 15 days. A hearing will be held before an ALJ of the Occupational Safety and Health Review Commission, who will issue a decision. The ALJ's decision is appealable to the Review Commission; the decision of the Review Commission is appealable to the federal court of appeals.

Mine Safety and Health Act (MSHA)

What It Does: Regulates workplace safety and health.

Who Is Covered: Employers engaged in the mining industry.

Where to Find It in the Law Books: 30 U.S. Code, secs. 8-01–8-78.

Who Enforces It: The Mine Safety and Health Administration (**MSHA**) has exclusive authority for enforcing the law. Individuals cannot file private lawsuits.

Where to Find More Information: Office of Information and Public Affairs, Mine Safety and Health Administration, Department of Labor, Room 601, 4015 Wilson Boulevard, Arlington, VA 22203.

Going to the MSHA: The enforcement process is substantially the same as that under OSHA.

PENSION AND WELFARE BENEFITS

Employee Retirement Income Security Act (ERISA)

What It Does: Regulates employee pension and welfare benefit plans.

Who Is Covered: Private sector employers whose business affects interstate commerce or whose pension and welfare plans are "qualified" under the federal tax laws.

Where to Find It in the Law Books: 29 U.S. Code, secs. 1001–1461.

Where to Find More Information: Department of Labor, Pension and Welfare Benefits Administration, 200 Constitution Avenue, N.W., Washington, DC 20210. Publications containing information concerning rights and duties under ERISA can be obtained by calling (202) 219-8921. The Pension Rights Center, 918 16th Street, N.W., Suite 704, Washington, DC 20006, and the American Association of Retired Persons, 601 E Street, N.W., Washington, DC 20049, are both organizations with information concerning pension rights under ERISA.

Who Enforces It: The Secretary of Labor has the responsibility to investigate violations of ERISA and can file a lawsuit to enforce the statute. Individual employees can also file lawsuits to enforce their rights under ERISA.

Going to Court: Employees alleging violations of ERISA with respect to the payment of benefits are required to use any dispute resolution procedures contained in the pension plan before filing a lawsuit. Any other violations of ERISA may be brought directly in federal court. Individuals are not required to file administrative charges before filing a lawsuit. The statute of limitations for filing a suit is six years from the date of the unlawful act, or three years from the date plaintiff had actual knowledge of the violations, whichever is earlier.

If You Win: Available remedies are injunctive relief and make-whole remedies.

OTHER TERMS OF EMPLOYMENT

Worker Adjustment and Retraining Notification Act (WARN)

What It Does: Requires employers to give advance notice of plant closings or mass layoffs.

Who Is Covered: Private sector employers with 100 or more employees.

Where to Find It in the Law Books: 29 U.S. Code, secs. 2102–2109.

Who Enforces It: Individual workers, unions, or a unit of local government may file a suit in federal district court to enforce the law.

Going to Court: There are no administrative prerequisites to filing a lawsuit. The deadline for filing a lawsuit is based on the most closely analogous state statute of limitations; this can vary anywhere from two years to six years.

If You Win: Successful plaintiffs are entitled to back pay for each day the law was violated, up to a maximum of 60 days, and the court may award reasonable attorney's fees.

Family and Medical Leave Act (FMLA)

What It Does: Requires employers to grant employees unpaid leave of absence for childbirth and serious health conditions. It also requires employers to reinstate an employee who had a leave of absence to his or her previous, or a substantially equivalent, job.

Who Is Covered: Private sector employers that employ 50 or more employees and public sector employers.

Where to Find It in the Law Books: 29 U.S. Code, secs. 2601, 2611–2619.

Where to Find More Information: Office of the Administrator, Wage and Hour Division, Department of Labor, Room S-3502, 200 Constitution Avenue, N.W., Washington, DC 20210.

Who Enforces It: The secretary of labor has the authority to investigate complaints of violations and can institute a lawsuit to enforce the statute. Individuals can file a complaint alleging a violation of the FMLA with the local office of the Wage and Hour Division of the

Department of Labor. Individual employees also have the right to sue their employer for violations of the law.

Going to Court: Individual employees may file suit directly in federal or state court. Employees can file charges with the Department of Labor, but this is not required. The statute of limitations for filing a lawsuit is two years.

INDEX

AARP (American Association of Retired Persons), 160
accommodation, reasonable, 22, 29, 55–56
accrued wages, 90
activity:
 concerted, 108
 illegal, 109
ADA, *see* Americans with Disabilities Act
ADEA, *see* Age Discrimination in Employment Act
adjudication stage, 143
administrative agency procedures, 145–47
administrative law judge (ALJ), 143, 167
advance notice, of family leave, 54
adverse employment actions, 112
adverse-impact discrimination, 17, 18–19, 38
advertising, of jobs, 24–26
affirmative action, 36–38
affirmative-action plan (AAP), 36–38
age, retirement, 100, 104
Age Discrimination in Employment Act (ADEA), 7, 9, 160–61
 and BFOQ, 20
 and discharge, 79, 81
 enforcement of, 160
 and health insurance, 69
 information sources on, 160
 and layoffs, 87–88
 remedies under, 161
 and retirement, 88–89
AIDS/HIV testing, 36
aliens, unauthorized, 15–16
ALJ (administrative law judge), 143, 167
American Association of Retired Persons (AARP), 160
Americans with Disabilities Act (ADA), Title I, 7, 9, 161–62
 disability, defined, 151–52
 and discharge, 79, 81
 enforcement of, 161–62

and essential functions, 23
and health insurance, 70–71
and hiring process, 29–31, 33–36
and hours worked, 55–56
information sources on, 161
and job requirements, 23–24
and personnel files, 60
protected class in, 149–50
remedies under, 162
and undue hardship, 30
American Workplace, Office of, 171
antidiscrimination laws, 7, 154–67
 ADA, 161–62
 ADEA, 160–61
 Civil Rights Act, 154–58
 discharge and, 79–80
 executive orders, 166–67
 in government employment, 128
 impact of, 41
 IRCA, 165–66
 Rehabilitation Act, 162–63
 remedying your loss under, 158–59
 Section 1981, 158–59
 Section 1983, 159–60
 USERRA, 163–65
 see also discrimination
anti-retaliation laws, 80–81, 91
application forms, 25–26, 85
arbitration:
 in government employment, 129
 of grievances, 119–20
 of internal complaints, 140–42
 of pension claims, 103
arbitrators, 120
association, freedom of, 132–33

background checks, 31–33
balancing test, 131
bankruptcy law, 65
bargaining power, of unions, 106
bargaining units, 115–16
benefits, noncash, 43
BFOQ (bona fide occupational qualifications), 20

181

blacklisting, 91
boycots, secondary, 124
breaks in service, 100–101

case law, 4
child labor laws, 14–15, 172–73
citizens, intending, 16
citizenship, defined, 151
Civil Rights Act (1964), Title VII of, 7, 9, 154–58
  and arbitration agreements, 140
  and BFOQ, 20
  definition of terms of, 149–51
  and discharge, 79, 81, 91
  and discipline, 66–67
  and dress codes, 62
  enforcement of, 155–57
  and English-only rules, 62
  and harassment, 57–60
  and health insurance, 68–69
  and hiring halls, 125
  and hours worked, 55
  information sources on, 155
  lawyers appointed for, 144–45
  protected class in, 149–50
  and references, 91
  remedies under, 157–58
  and unions, see unions
civil service laws, 4, 130
  and collective bargaining, 129
  and discharge, 79
COBRA (Consolidated Omnibus Budget Reconciliation Act), 69
collective bargaining agreements, 4, 78, 115–22
  and arbitration procedure, 119–20
  and duty to bargain, 118
  and government employment, 129
  and grievance procedure, 119–21
  impasse in, 117
  just cause clauses in, 118–19
  law of the shop in, 118
  mandatory subjects of, 118
  no-strike clauses in, 124
  union security clauses in, 121–22
commerce, instrumentalities of, 152–53
common law, 12–13
common-law compensatory damages, 158
community of interest, 116
company personnel handbooks, see handbooks
comparable worth theory, 49

compelling interest, 134
compensation for injury, see workers' compensation laws
compensatory damages, 157–58
concerted activity, 108
conciliation, 146, 156
conduct, group, 108
Consolidated Omnibus Budget Reconciliation Act (COBRA), 69
Constitution, U.S.:
  and balancing test, 131
  and drug testing, 134
  and due process, 136–37
  and employee searches, 133–35
  Fifth Amendment, 135–37
  First Amendment, 131–33
  Fourth Amendment, 133–35
  and freedom of association, 132–33
  and freedom of speech, 131–32
  and government employment, 130–37
  and privacy rights, 136
  and self-incrimination, 135
Consumer Credit Protection Act, and garnishments, 50–51
consumer reports, 32
contingency fee arrangements, 145
contingent workers, 6
contractors, independent, 4–5, 6
contracts:
  employment, 4, 41–42, 78
  unilateral or implied, 40, 84, 140–41
covenants not to compete, 92–93

Davis-Bacon Act, 45, 174
decertification elections, 114–15
defamation, 32
  defined, 91
  and intentional infliction of emotional distress, 92
  qualified privilege defense to, 91
de minimis costs, 22
democratic majoritarian principle, 115
depositions, 147–48
direct injuries, 158
disabilities:
  and ADA, see Americans with Disabilities Act
  definition of term, 151–52
  and hiring process, 23–24, 29–31, 33–34

job-induced, 74
and job requirements, 23–24
leave time and, 55–56
qualified, 152
reasonable accommodation of, 22,
29, 55–56
and Rehabilitation Act, 7, 151–52,
162–63
and testing, 33–34
disability insurance, social security,
76–77
Disability Rights Center, 161
Disability Rights Education and
Defense Fund, 161
disabling medical condition, 77
discharge, 78–85
and antidiscrimination laws, 79–80
and anti–retaliation laws, 80–81, 91
arbitrary, 79
and grievances, 79
for just cause, 78–79, 118–19, 130
vs. layoff, 85–86
and mitigation, 89–90
and opposition activity, 81
and participation activity, 81
of protected classes, 80
and references, 90–92
and state laws, 82–85
and whistle-blower laws, 81–82
discipline:
employee, 65–68
and just cause clauses, 118–19
disclaimers, express, 40
discrimination, 17–21
adverse-impact, 17, 18–19, 38
and employment agencies, 38
and executive orders, 166–67
and harassment, 57–60
intentional, 17, 18, 38
and job requirements, 19
laws against, see antidiscrimination
laws
and protected categories, 17
and Section 1981, 158–59
and union activity, 169
disqualifying events, 94
distress, intentional infliction of, 92
distribution of literature, 110–13
dress codes, 62, 112
Drug-Free Workplace Act, 17
drug-testing laws, 16–17, 35–36
and compelling interest, 134
and Fourth Amendment, 133–34

and privacy, 61–62
reasonable suspicion in, 134
due process:
and Fifth Amendment, 136–37
and liberty interests, 136
and property interests, 136
duty to bargain, 118

economic strikes, 122
EEOC, see Equal Employment
Opportunities Commission
elections:
interference with, 133
time off for voting in, 56–57
union, 113–15
Employee Polygraph Protection Act
(EPPA), 8, 12, 34–35, 67–68
Employee Retirement Income Security
Act (ERISA), 8, 11, 98–103, 177
benefit accrual in, 98–99
and discharge, 79
and 401(k) plans, 98
and government employment, 128
participation and, 98
preemption of, 98
employees:
bankruptcy law and, 65
in community of interest, 116
vs. contingent workers, 6
discipline of, 65–68
and due process, 136–37
employers' economic power over, 83
engaged in interstate commerce,
152–53
and Fourth Amendment searches,
133–35
of government, see government
employment
hiring of, see hiring process
immigrant, 8, 15–16, 165–67
vs. independent contractors, 4–5, 6
monitoring of, 63–64
notice posting and, 5–7
off-duty conduct of, 64
political activity of, 65, 133
privacy of, see privacy
private sector, 149
public sector, 149
quitting, 89
reasonable accommodation of, 22,
29, 55–56
rights of, 107–13, 140
and unions, see unions

employees at will, 3
  and application forms, 85
  and discharge, 78
  and just cause clause, 118
  and state laws, 82–85
employers:
  adverse employment actions by, 112
  bargaining in good faith by, 117
  economic power of, 83
  government as, *see* government
    employment
  lawyers retained by, 143
  legitimate interest of, 109
  primary, 124
  private sector, 149
  public sector, 149
  rights of, 110–13
  secondary, 124
  and unions, *see* unions
employment:
  ending of, *see* ending employment
  terms of, *see* terms and conditions of
    employment
employment agencies, 38
  hiring halls as, 125
employment contracts, 4, 41–42, 78
employment laws, 154–79; *see also*
    specific laws
ending employment, 78–96
  accrued wages in, 90
  being fired, 78–85; *see also*
    discharge
  being laid off, 85–88; *see also*
    layoffs
  and covenants not to compete,
    92–93
  fair warning of, 86
  mitigation in, 89–90
  quitting, 89, 94–95
  references in, 90–92
  retirement, 88–89
  and unemployment compensation,
    93–96
enforcement, 138–48
  adjudication stage of, 143
  administrative agency procedures,
    145–47
  administrative law judge for, 143
  and arbitration, 141–42
  court procedures in, 147–48
  and implied contract theory, 140–41
  internal complaint procedures,
    138–42

investigations in, 146
  lawyers for, 142–47
  and mediation, 139
  and personnel handbooks, 140–41
English-only rules, 62
EPA (Equal Pay Act), 7, 49, 173
EPPA (Employee Polygraph Protection
    Act), 8, 12, 34–35, 67–68
Equal Employment Opportunities
    Commission (EEOC):
  and ADA, 161–62
  address of, 155
  and ADEA, 160–61
  and application forms, 26
  and arbitration agreements, 140
  and Civil Rights Act, 155–57
  and conciliation, 156
  and essential functions, 23
  filing charges with, 156
  and health insurance, 71
  and Rehabilitation Act, 162
  and right to sue letter, 156
Equal Pay Act (EPA), 7, 49, 173
ERISA, *see* Employee Retirement
    Income Security Act
essential functions, 23
ethnicity:
  and Section 1981, 158–59
  see also discrimination
evidence, direct and indirect, 18
exclusive hiring halls, 125
executive orders:
  11,141, 166
  11,246, 38
  12,086, 166
  12,989, 16, 166
  enforcement of, 166–67
express disclaimers, 40

FAA (Federal Aviation Administration),
    52–53
Fair Credit Reporting Act (FCRA), 32
Fair Labor Standards Act (FLSA), 7,
    172–73
  and child labor, 14–15, 172
  enforcement of, 172
  information source on, 172
  and interstate commerce, 152–53
  and layoffs, 87
  remedies under, 173
  and wages, 42–45, 48
Family and Medical Leave Act (FMLA),
    8–9, 12, 53–54, 178–79

FCRA (Fair Credit Reporting Act), 32
Federal Aviation Administration (FAA),
  52–53
Federal Labor Relations Act (FLRA),
  128–29, 170
federal laws, 7–9
  definition of terms in, 149–53
  locating, 155
  state laws and, 11–13
  see also specific laws
Federal Service Impasses Panel, 170
fiduciaries, 101, 127
Fifth Amendment of U.S. Constitution,
  135–37
First Amendment of U.S. Constitution,
  131–33
FLRA (Federal Labor Relations Act),
  128–29, 170
FLSA, *see* Fair Labor Standards Act
FMLA (Family and Medical Leave Act),
  8–9, 12, 53–54, 178–79
401(k) plans, 98–99
Fourth Amendment of U.S.
  Constitution, 133–35

garnishments, 50–51
gender:
  defined, 151
  and EPA, 7, 49, 173
good cause:
  discharge for, 78–79, 118–19, 130
  quitting for, 94
government employment, 128–37
  and antidiscrimination laws, 128
  balancing test in, 131
  civil service laws of, 130
  and collective bargaining, 129
  constitutional protections in,
    130–37
  and discharge, 79
  and drug testing, 133–34
  and due process, 136–37
  and EEO counselors, 157
  and employee monitoring, 63–64
  and employee searches, 133–35
  and freedom of association, 132–33
  and freedom of speech, 131–32
  labor-management relations in,
    128–30
  and liberty interest, 136–37
  and privacy, 136
  and property interest, 136–37
  and Rehabilitation Act, 162–63

and self-incrimination, 135
and strikes, 129
whistle-blower laws and, 82
grievances, 119–21
  arbitration of, 119–20
  and discharge, 79
  procedures for, 119, 140–41
group conduct, 108

handbooks:
  and binding contracts, 85
  and enforcement, 140–41
  personnel, 4, 39–40
  specific language of, 84
harassment, 57–60
  hostile environment, 57–58
  prevention of, 58
  quid pro quo, 58–59
  same-sex, 60
  and strict liability, 59–60
  unwelcome, 59
  victim actions in, 59
Hatch Act, 133
Hazard Communication Standard, 72
health insurance, 68–71
  and changing jobs, 70–71
  and preexisting conditions, 70
Health Insurance Portability and
  Accountability Act, 70–71
hiring halls, 125
hiring process, 14–38
  advertising in, 24–26
  affirmative action in, 36–38
  aliens and, 15–16
  application forms, 25–26
  BFOQ in, 20
  biased questions in, 28
  child labor laws, 14–15
  disabilities and, 23–24, 29–31,
    33–34
  discrimination in, 17–21
  drug testing, 16–17
  employment agencies and, 38
  interviews in, 27–29
  job requirements and, 23–24
  licenses and, 17
  privacy and, 31
  references in, 31–33
  scheduling requirements and, 22
  testing in, 33–36
HIV/AIDS testing, 36
hostile environment harassment, 57–58
Hours of Service Act, 52

hours worked, 52–53
    and advance notice, 54
    day's work for a day's pay, 111
    and leaves, 53–57
    and overtime, 45–48, 172–73
    and wages, 43–44
    and working time, 110

illness:
    compensable, 75
    job-related, 74–77
immigrant workers, 8
    and executive orders, 166–67
    intending citizens, 16
    Special Counsel office, 165
    unauthorized, 15–16
Immigration and Nationality Act, 16
Immigration Reform and Control Act
        (IRCA), 8, 165–66
    citizenship, defined, 151
    and employment agencies, 38
    enforcement of, 165
    Form 19 of, 15–16
    information sources on, 165
    national origin, defined, 150
    remedies under, 166
impasse, in collective bargaining, 117
impasse resolution procedures, 129
implied contracts, 40, 84, 140–41
incentive packages, 87, 88–89
independent contractors, 4–5, 6
indirect injuries, 158
Individual Retirement Accounts (IRAs),
        100
injunctions, 93
injunctive relief, 157, 158
injury:
    compensable, 75, 158
    job-related, 74–77
instrumentalities of commerce,
        152–53
insurance:
    health, 68–71
    pensions and, 102
    social security disability, 76–77
intentional discrimination, 17, 18, 38
intentional infliction of emotional
        distress, 92
interference, intentional, 91
intermittent strikes, 124
internal complaint procedures, 138–42
interstate commerce, employees engaged
        in, 152–53

Interstate Reciprocal Benefit Payment
        Plan, 96
interviews:
    biased questions in, 28
    in hiring process, 27–29
    objectivity in, 27
    oral promises in, 85
    written record of, 27–28
investigative consumer reports, 32
IRAs (Individual Retirement Accounts),
        100
IRCA, see Immigration Reform and
        Control Act

job descriptions, 24–26
job requirements, 19, 20–21, 23–24
joint and survivor annuity benefits, 102
Jury Systems Improvements Act, 12, 56
just cause:
    for discharge, 78–79, 118–19, 130
    quitting for, 94
Justice Department, U.S., and
        immigration law, 165

labor and employment laws, 154–79
    employment discrimination laws,
        154–67
    other terms of employment, 178–79
    pension and welfare benefits, 177
    remedies under, 158–59
    union-management laws, 167–72
    wage and hour laws, 172–75
    workplace safety laws, 175–76
Labor Department, U.S.:
    Office of American Workplace in,
        171
    Office of Labor-Management
        Standards in, 171
    Pension and Welfare Benefits
        Administration of, 177
    and VETS, 164
    Wage and Hour Division of,
        172–73, 174, 178
Labor-Management Reporting and
        Disclosure Act (LMRDA),
        126–27, 171–72
Labor-Management Standards (LMS),
        Office of, 171
Landrum-Griffin Act (LMRDA),
        126–27
law:
    bankruptcy, 65
    case, 4

common, 12–13
effects on workplace of, 3–13
federal, definitions of terms in, 149–53
personal injury, 31
of the shop, 118
tort, 31, 91
see also specific laws
lawsuits, 147–48
right to sue letters and, 156
and statutes of limitation, 157
lawyers, 142–47
court-appointed, 144–45
and court procedures, 147–48
and depositions, 147–48
employer retention of, 143
fees of, 145
finding, 144–45
layoffs, 85–88
discharges vs., 85–86
mass, 86, 87
notice of, 87
and plant closings, 86
seniority and, 86
and unemployment compensation, 94
waivers in, 87–88
League of United Latin American Citizens, 165
leave time, 53–57
advance notice of, 54
for serious medical condition, 54
in uniformed services, 56
for voting in elections, 56–57
legitimate employer interest, 109
liability:
and harassment, 59–60
and workers' compensation, 74
liberty interests, 136–37
licenses, work, 17
lie detector tests, 8, 34–35, 67–68
liquidated damages, 161
litigation, 147–48
LMRDA (Labor-Management Reporting and Disclosure Act), 126–27, 171–72
LMS (Office of Labor-Management Standards), 171

majoritarian principle, 115
make-whole remedies, 157, 158, 159
manager, defined, 107
manuals:
and binding contracts, 85

and enforcement, 140–41
personnel, 4, 39–40
specific language of, 84
mass layoffs, 86, 87
mediation, 139
in government employment, 129
National Mediation Board, 169
mediators, 139
medical condition, disabling, 77
medical tests, 35
Mental Health Law Project, 161
men and women, equal pay for, 7, 49, 173
merit system laws, 129
Merit Systems Protection Board (MSPB), 165
Mexican American legal Defense and Educational Fund, 165
Mine Safety and Health Act (MSHA), 176
misconduct, 95, 134–35
misrepresentation, negligent, 91
mitigation, 89–90
Motor Carriers Act, 52

National Association of Working Women, 173
National Labor Relations Act (NLRA), 8, 167–69
and arbitration agreements, 140
and discharge, 79
and dress codes, 62
and employee rights, 107
enforcement of, 168–69
and government employment, 128
information source on, 168
and preemption, 11
and privacy, 61, 63–64
remedies under, 169
state-law versions of, 10
and unemployment compensation, 95
and unions, 106–27; *see also* unions
National Labor Relations Board (NLRB), 114, 168
National Mediation Board (NMB), 169
National Organization for Women, 173
National Railroad Adjustment Board (NRAB), 169
National Veterans Legal Services Project, 164
negligent misrepresentation, 91

NLRA, *see* National Labor Relations Act
NMB (National Mediation Board), 169
nonexclusive hiring halls, 125
no-strike clauses, 124
notice posting, 5–7

occupational diseases, 75
Occupational Safety and Health Act, 8, 72–73, 175–76
  anti-retaliation clause of, 82
  and government employment, 128
  and medical records, 61
Occupational Safety and Health Administration (OSHA), 175–76
OFCCP (Office of Federal Contract Compliance), 162–63, 166
off-duty conduct, 64
Omnibus Crime Control and Safe Streets Act, Title III of, and wiretapping, 63
opposition activity, 81
OSHA (Occupational Safety and Health Administration), 175–76
overtime:
  and FLSA, 172–73
  and wages, 45–48
  and workweek, 45

participation activity, 81
part-time (contingent) workers, 6
payroll records, 48
pension and welfare benefits laws, 177
Pension Benefit Guaranty Corporation (PBGC), 102
pensions, 8, 97–103
  administration of funds of, 101
  benefit accrual in, 98–99
  and breaks in service, 100–101
  claims for, 103
  defined-benefit plans, 97, 102
  defined-contribution plans, 97
  ERISA, 98–103
  fiduciaries of, 101
  401(k) plans, 98–99
  funding of, 101
  joint and survivor provisions of, 101–2
  participation in, 98
  qualified joint and survivor annuity benefits of, 102
  reporting and disclosure of, 103
  rolling over funds in, 100

summary plan description of, 103
  taxes and, 100
  termination of, 102–3
  vesting in, 99–100
Personal Earnings and Benefit Statement Form, 105
personal injury law, 31
personality tests, 35
personnel files, 60–61
personnel manuals, *see* manuals
plant closings:
  and layoffs, 86
  and unemployment compensation, 94
political activity of employees, 65, 133
preemption, 11
pregnancy, and health insurance, 68–69
primary employers, 124
privacy, 62–63
  and drug testing, 61–62
  of medical records, 61
  and off-duty conduct, 64
  and personnel files, 60–61
  protection of, 31
  reasonable expectation of, 134
  right of, 136
  and searches, 64, 133–35
  and wiretapping, 63
Privacy Act, 60–61
private sector employees, 149
private sector employers, 149
probable cause, and searches, 64, 135
productivity, and union activity, 111
proper cause:
  for discharge, 78–79, 118–19, 130
  quitting for, 94
property interests, and due process, 136–37
protected classes, 149–50
public policy, 82–83
public sector employees, 149
public sector employers, 149
punitive damages, 157–58, 159

qualified disabilities, 152
qualified privilege defense, 91
quarters, of disability coverage, 76
quid pro quo harassment, 58–59
quitting, 89
  good cause for, 94
  reasonable person perspective, 94–95
  and unemployment compensation, 94

race:
    defined, 150
    and Section 1981, 158–59
    see also Civil Rights Act;
        discrimination
Railway Labor Act (RLA), 126, 169–70
reasonable accommodation, 22, 29,
    55–56
reasonable expectation of privacy, 134
reasonable person perspective, 94–95
reasonable suspicion, 134
references, 31–33
    and ending of employment, 90–92
    safe, 92
Rehabilitation Act, 7, 151–52, 162–63
relief, injunctive, 157, 158
religion:
    defined, 150
    and scheduling, 22
remedies, types of, 158–59
reputation, and liberty interests, 136
Request for Correction of Earnings
    Record (Form OAR-7008), 105
retirement, 97–105
    mandatory, 88
    and pensions, 97–103
    planning for, 105
    and social security, 104–5
    voluntary, 88–89
retirement age, 100, 104
rights:
    constitutional, see Constitution, U.S.
    of employees, 107–10, 140
    of employers, 110–13
    enforcement of, see enforcement
right to sue letters, 156
RLA (Railway Labor Act), 126, 169–70

sabotage, and strikes, 123–24
safety, 8, 72–73, 175–76
same-sex harassment, 60
schedule, payment, 74
scheduling requirements, 22, 29
searches:
    and Fourth Amendment, 133–35
    and privacy, 64, 134
    and probable cause, 64, 135
secondary boycotts, 124
secondary employers, 124
Section 1981, 158–59
Section 1983, 159–60
self-incrimination, 135
serious medical condition, 54

Service Contract Act, 45, 174–75
service letter acts, 90
sex:
    defined, 151
    and EPA, 7, 49, 173
shop, law of, 118
sit-down strikes, 124
smoking, restrictions on, 62
social security, 104–5
    disability insurance system, 76–77
    and normal retirement age, 104
    Personal Earnings and Benefit
        Statement Form, 105
Social Security Administration (SSA),
    77
solicitation, 110–13
solidarity, 123
Special Counsel for Immigration-
    Related Unfair Employment
    Practices, 165
speech, freedom of, 131–32
state laws, 9–11
    civil service, 130
    and compensatory damages, 158
    and employment at will, 82–85
    federal laws and, 11–13
    and government employment, 129
    and Hatch Act, 133
    public policy exceptions, 82–83
    regulatory, in absence of federal law,
        11, 12–13
    as supplement or extension, 11, 12
    and unions, 11, 106, 121
    workers' compensation, 75
states, and unemployment
    compensation, 93–96
statutes, 4
statutes of limitation, 157
statutory compensatory damages, 158
strikes, 122–24
    conduct during, 123–24
    economic, 122
    and government employment, 129
    and impasse resolution procedures,
        129
    intermittent, 124
    and no-strike clauses, 124
    purposes of, 122–23
    reinstatement after, 122–23
    sit-down, 124
    and solidarity, 123
    sympathy, 123
    timing of, 124

strikes (*cont'd*)
    and unemployment compensation, 95
    unfair labor practice, 122–23
supervisors:
    defined, 107
    in government employment, 129
sympathy strikers, 123

telephone device for the deaf (TDD), 29
telephones, wiretapping and, 63
temp (contingent) workers, 6
terms and conditions of employment, 39–77
    in collective bargaining agreement, 118
    discipline, 65–68
    dress codes, 62
    drug testing, 61–62
    employer decisions of, 39–41
    English-only rules, 62
    government employees and, 63–64, 129
    in handbooks, 39–40
    harassment, 57–60
    health insurance, 68–71
    hours worked, 52–57
    illness and injury, job-related, 74–77
    law's impact on, 41–42
    personnel files, 60–61
    privacy, 62–65
    safety, 72–73
    smoking restrictions, 62
    surveillance, 63–64
    telephone privacy, 63
    wages, 42–52
    written contracts, 41
testing:
    in hiring process, 33–36
    polygraph, 8, 34–35, 67–68
    see also drug-testing laws
tips, and wages, 44–45
Title I, ADA, *see* Americans with Disabilities Act
Title III, Omnibus Crime Control and Safe Streets Act, 63
Title VII, *see* Civil Rights Act
tort law, 31, 91
Transportation Department, U.S., 52
trespass rule, 111

undue hardship, 22, 30
unemployment compensation, 93–96

unemployment insurance laws, 10
unfair labor practice strikes, 122–23
uniformed services, 56
Uniformed Services Employment and Reemployment Rights Act (USERRA), 8, 163–65
    and discharge, 79–80
    enforcement of, 164–65
    and health insurance, 69
    informaton sources on, 164
    leave time and, 56
    and pensions, 100
    remedies under, 165
unilateral (implied) contracts, 40, 84, 140–41
union-management laws, 167–72
    FLRA, 170
    LMRDA, 171–72
    NLRA, 167–69
    RLA, 169–70
unions, 106–27
    acting without, 108
    and adverse employment actions, 112
    and arbitration, 119–20
    authorization cards, 108
    bargaining power of, 106
    coercive actions of, 113
    and collective bargaining agreements, 4, 78, 115–22
    decertification elections, 114–15
    and democratic majoritarian principle, 115
    and discrimination, 169
    and distribution of literature, 110–13
    and dress codes, 62, 112
    and drug testing, 61–62
    election procedures of, 113–15
    and employee rights, 107–13
    fair representation by, 116, 121, 125
    fair share payments to, 121
    and government employment, 129
    and grievances, 79, 119–21
    and hiring halls, 125
    internal affairs of, 126–27
    legislation and, 8, 9–10
    and LMRDA, 126–27, 171–72
    political rights within, 126
    reasonableness of, 116
    and religious beliefs, 121
    right to form and join, 108

and RLA, 169–70
and secondary boycotts, 124
and security clauses, 121–22
service fees of, 121
solicitation for, 110–13
and state law, 11, 106, 121
and strikes, 122–24
surveillance of activities of, 63–64
and trespass rule, 111
see also National Labor Relations
Act
U.S. Code, locating federal laws in, 155
USERRA, see Uniformed Services
Employment and Reemployment
Rights Act

vandalism, and strikes, 123–24
vesting, 99–100
Veterans of Foreign Wars, 164
VETS (Veterans' Employment and
Training Service), 164

wage and hour laws, 172–75
Davis-Bacon Act, 174
Equal Pay Act, 173
FLSA, 172–73
Service Contract Act, 174–75
Walsh-Healy Act, 174
wage payment statutes, 90
wages, 7, 42–52
accrued, 90
for administrative employees, 47–48
in coin of the realm, 43
and comparable worth, 49
for computer professionals, 46
and ending of employment, 90
for executives, 47
garnishments and, 50–51
minimum wage laws, 42–45
and noncash benefits, 43
other laws, 45
for outside salespeople, 46
overtime, 45–48

and payroll records, 48
prevailing, 45
for professionals, 47
and retail commissions, 45–46
setting rates of, 48–49
and tips, 44–45
youth subminimum, 42
Wagner Act, see National Labor
Relations Act
waivers, 87–88
Walsh-Healey Public Contracts Act, 45,
174
WARN (Worker Adjustment and
Retraining Notification Act), 8,
81, 86, 178
whistle-blower laws, 81–82
Whistleblower Protection Act, 82
wiretapping, 63
women, equal pay for, 7, 49, 173
Worker Adjustment and Retraining
Notification Act (WARN), 8, 81,
86, 178
workers, see employees
workers' compensation laws, 10, 74–77
collecting benefits of, 76
contingency fee arrangements for,
145
death and permanent disability, 74
payment schedule in, 74
and social security disability, 76–77
strict liability under, 74
working time, 110
workplace rights, enforcement of, see
enforcement
workplace safety laws:
MSHA, 176
OSHA and, 175–76
work-related misconduct, 134–35
work standards, 19
Wrongful Discharge from Employment
Act, 79

youth subminimum wage, 42

BARBARA J. FICK is an associate professor of law at Notre Dame Law School, specializing in labor employment law, and dispute resolution. She is on the board of editors of the journal *International Contributions to Labour Studies,* and is a member of the George Higgins Labor Research Center at Notre Dame. She has written numerous scholarly articles on labor and employment law, and has delivered scholarly papers and lectures in Hungary and Poland, as well as in the United States. She has also served as a mediator and arbitrator in labor relations cases, and has been an expert witness in such cases. Before coming to Notre Dame she was a field attorney at the National Labor Relations Board.